TABLE OF CONTENTS

Page

LIST OF TABLES

iv

LIST OF FIGURES

ACRONYMS

APC	Armored Personnel Carrier
APOD	Aerial Port of Debarkation
BCTP	Battle Command Training Program
BF	Breach Facility
CACTF	Combined Arms Collective Training Facility
CAMTF	Combined Arms MOUT Task Force
CMTC	Combat Maneuver Training Center
COE	Contemporary Operating Environment
CONUS	Continental United States
CTC	Combat Training Center
DOD	Department of Defense
DOTMLF	Doctrine, Organization, Training, Material, Leadership, People, Facilities
DTLOMS	Doctrine, Training, Leader, Organization, Material, and Soldiers
HMMWV	Highly Mobile Multi-Wheeled Vehicle
IFV	Infantry Fighting Vehicle
JFCOM	Joint Forces Command
JRTC	Joint Readiness Training Center
MOUT	Military Operations on Urban Terrain
NTC	National Training Center
OneSAF	One Semi-automated Force
ROE	Rules of Engagement
RPG	Rocket Propelled Grenade
RPV	Remotely Piloted Vehicle
SH	Shoot House
SNA	Somali National Alliance
SPOD	Sea Port of Debarkation
TFR	Task Force Ranger
TTP	Technique, Tactics, and Procedures
UAC	Urban Assault Course
UO	Urban Operations

CHAPTER 1
INTRODUCTION
Statement of the Problem, Background and Significance

Recent UN forecasts predict that 85 percent of the world's population will reside in urban areas by the year 2025.[1] As the world trend towards urbanization increases, the military significance of cities is likely to increase proportionally. Urbanized areas, themselves, may become significant sources of future conflict. This dramatic shift of the world's population will only serve to increase the need to create military capabilities adequate to successfully execute urban operations across the full spectrum.

While the cold war doctrine emphasized "city avoidance", the contemporary and future threat environment may make operations in cities impossible to avoid. Learning from the demonstration of America's technological superiority on the open field of battle during Operation Desert Storm, contemporary and future enemies hope to use the complexity of urban terrain as a means to counter US advantages. American experiences in Mogadishu and Russian experiences in Grozny serve as an example of less capable forces using urban terrain asymmetrically to even the balance of power against technologically superior military forces.

Since the Cold War, the US Army has focused much of its urban training efforts to deal with urban operations at the lower end of the threat spectrum. The success of this investment has been demonstrated in such operations as those conducted in Haiti, Bosnia, and Kosovo. But has the US Army successfully adjusted to prepare for the increasingly likely, higher end of the spectrum of urban conflict? Or has it maintained a focus on fighting in the less-likely symmetrical warfare of the open field?

---

[1] Government Accounting Office, *Military Capabilities: Focused Attention Needed to Prepare U.S. Forces for Combat in Urban Areas,* GAO/NSIAD-00-63NI (February, 2000): 6.

Research Questions

The primary research question is as follows: Is the US Army adequately preparing for contemporary and future urban operations?

The secondary and tertiary questions are as follows:

1. What is the urban threat and how likely is urban combat in the future?

2. What is the state of our UO doctrine?

    a. Is our UO doctrine joint, combined arms, and does it cover the full-spectrum of operations?

3. What is the state of our urban warfare training?

    a. Does our UO training include joint forces, is it combined arms in nature, and does it cover the full spectrum of operations?

    b. How often and at what level are units conducting UO training?

        i. Home station?

        ii. Combat Training Centers?

        iii. Simulations?

    c. Does UO receive adequate emphasis within Army commands?

4. Are units resourced with adequate UO training facilities and UO equipment?

Scope

The scope of this monograph will include an examination of the urban environment, current status of UO doctrine, training, and resourcing of the Army. It will not however, examine organization and force structure issues within the Army with regards to the execution of urban operations. While these are extremely important issues, they are beyond the scope and purpose of this monograph. The scope of this monograph will also be limited to examining primarily the Army branch of service and will not extend its research to cover the performance, needs and capabilities in UO by other branches of service.

Definition of Key Terms

The literature uses the terms "urban combat" and "fighting in cities" and "urban operations" (UO) interchangeably. The doctrinal term, urban operations, is a new doctrinal term that replaces the term Military Operations in Urban Terrain or MOUT. According to the new FM 3-06, UO are operations across the full spectrum of conflict that occur in an urban environment. The environment consists of complex terrain, a concentration of population, and an infrastructure of systems that form an operational environment in which the Army will operate.[2] This is a significant change from previous doctrine, which viewed urban centers as simply unique terrain. The new term addresses not only the unique urban terrain, but expands its definition to encompass the unique environment of urban centers.

Methodology

This monograph uses primary and secondary sources gathered from historical records, books, pamphlets, periodicals, master's theses and monographs in order to answer the research question. Additionally it uses sources of information from the Department of the Army, Training and Doctrine Command, and the Combined Arms Command. In conjunction with personal interviews by the author, the monograph uses a series of surveys sent to various units ranging from brigade through company level throughout the Army to gather information concerning training and resourcing for urban warfare. The contents of these surveys are used to provide empirical data to further determine the level of proficiency to which our Army is training for UO, thus moving beyond mere speculation as to how prepared the Army is for urban warfare.

The monograph will review the urban threat and make a determination of what the Army must be prepared to face. Particularly it will examine lessons from both U.S. experience in Mogadishu and Russian experiences in Grozny.

---

[2] U.S. Army, FM 3-06 *Urban Operations*, (Washington, D.C.: Department of the Army, 2002), viii.

Next it will review the current state of our UO doctrine in an attempt to determine if it is joint and combined arms in nature as well as determine if it covers the full spectrum of possible urban operations.

The monograph will examine the Army's UO training to determine whether or not the Army is preparing sufficiently for contemporary and future urban threats. Specifically, it will attempt to ascertain how often units are conducting UO training, to what intensity, and does this training include joint forces, combined arms, as well as cover the entire spectrum of operations. It will address the level of emphasis UO receives in units based on the content of quarterly training guidance, unit mission essential task lists, and time dedicated to UO training.

Following the examination of training readiness, it will analyze the Army's resourcing of units in preparation for urban offensive operations to determine if units are appropriately resourced for urban combat. The analysis will cover the adequacy of UO training facilities in the Army, and the level of UO specific equipment provided to units enabling them to conduct UO training.

Finally the monograph will outline the findings and conclusions on whether or not our Army is adequately preparing for contemporary and future urban warfare, and provide recommendations to fix any problems identified in UO doctrine, training and resourcing.

CHAPTER 2

THE CONTEMPORARY AND FUTURE URBAN ENVIORNMENT

> Cities always have been centers of gravity, but they are now more magnetic than ever before…They concentrate people and power, communications and control, knowledge and capability, rendering all else peripheral. They are also the post-modern equivalent of jungles and mountains – citadels of the dispossessed and irreconcilable. A military unprepared for urban operations across the broad spectrum is unprepared for tomorrow.
>
> Ralph Peters, *Fighting for the Future*

> If you're fighting me, and you have this great Air Force and this great Navy with these precision weapons, I'm going to find a way for you not to use them. I'm going to fight you in the city so you're going to have to kill the city or kill me. Or I'm going to take refugees. I'm going to let you kill civilians and see how that flies on CNN. Doing that gives you a big problem.
>
> LTG (RET) Jay M. Garner, USA

Background

During the Cold War, U.S. Army doctrine stressed city avoidance in favor of fighting with large maneuver forces on the open plains of Europe. Cities slowed maneuver tempo and were to be bypassed; entered only as a last result. The Cold War is now over. In 1989, with the collapse of the Berlin Wall, we entered into a new era; one that we have been slow to fully understand and reticent to adapt to. Today our armed forces must be prepared to fight in what is called the contemporary operating environment (COE) across the full spectrum of conflict. This new environment will more likely involve our armed forces operating within urban complexes.

Urban Trends

It is difficult to read any book or article written in the past ten years on the topic of Urban Operations (formerly known as MOUT or military operations, urban terrain), without discovering a repeat of a common mantra; U.S. military involvement in urban operations is increasingly likely. What has changed in the world to create this increased likeliness of U.S. military involvement in urban operations?

5

Some point to the myriad of statistics that document the world's increased urbanization as a reason for the likeliness of involvement in urban operations. In the Government Accounting Office's (GAO) report titled *Focused Attention Needed to Prepare U.S. Forces for Combat in Urban Areas*, it states that half of the world's populations live in urban areas today. By 2015, that figure is expected to reach 75 percent, and by the year 2025, 85 percent of the world's population is expected to reside in an urban setting.[3]

	1950	1990	2015
"Million Cities" (Pop. >1 million)	**50**	**270**	**516**
"Mega cities" (Pop. > 8 million)	Worldwide: **2** Developing World: **0**	Worldwide: **21** Developing World: **16**	Worldwide: **33** Developing World: **27**

Table 1. Global Urban Population Trends[4]

An increased urban population is not the only cause for the growing likeliness of military involvement in cities, rather it is the dynamics this population influx into cities has created, particularly in developing countries. Driven by economic necessity, huge numbers of people are quitting the rural lifestyle of their ancestors and moving to cities worldwide. The number of cities with a current population of over one million in the developing world alone has grown from 34 in 1950, to 213 as of 1995.[5]

Mega cities are exploding in developing and underdeveloped nations; the United Nations estimates Mexico City to have 15.6 million people and Sao Palo, Brazil 16 million.[6] Explosive growth rates in earlier eras gave infrastructure a chance to keep pace, but now it is overwhelming the infrastructure of many cities. Cairo's population equals 15 million with an infrastructure to support only 2 million.[7]

---

[3] GAO, *Military Capabilities: Focused Attention Needed to Prepare U.S. Forces for Combat in Urban Areas*, 6,7.

[4] "A Concept for Future Military Operations on Urbanized Terrain," *Marine Corps Gazette* 81, no.10 (October 1997): A-1.

[5] Thomas X. Hammes, "Preparing for Today's Battlefield," *Marine Corps Gazette* 81, no. 7 (July 1997): 56.

[6] Ibid.

[7] Ibid.

This overburden of urban infrastructure creates more breakdowns in social order and control particularly among developing countries with fledgling democracies and weak central governments. Populations of different social classes within these urban complexes are thrust together as never before leading to further strife, as the "haves" are more visible than ever to a growing class of "have-nots". This is particularly true in an environment where there are surges in male youth population disaffected by unemployment, lack of resources, and loss of faith in the current governing system. Without the support structure of family and traditional sources of social control left behind in their rural settings, these urban populations in mega cities are more likely to disintegrate into disorder, chaos and violence.

Despite that urban centers are growing rapidly, their infrastructure is insufficient, and there is a greater chance for social disorder within in them, it does not necessarily translate into U.S. forces becoming more involved in urban operations. But cities by their very nature as focal points for populations, commerce, and government are likely points of interface between U.S. interests and the interests of foreign governments and non-state actors.[8]

Urban Operational Spectrum

What the urban statistics listed above portray is an environment that will require greater U.S. involvement at the lower end of the operational spectrum while conducting Stability and Support Operations (SASO). In the still-evolving post-Cold War security environment, cities have proven to be a locus for U.S. military involvement. Recent history already serves as a testament to this fact. City names like Port-au-Prince, Mogadishu, Tirana, Freetown, Monrovia, Brcko, and Kabul to name a few, are examples of the growing trend of our SASO involvement in urban operations.

These urban centers also provide safe-haven for current 4th generation warfare opponents; terrorists, insurgents, and trans-national criminal organizations. Such enemies have migrated to

---

[8] "A Concept for Future Military Operations on Urbanized Terrain," A-1.

large cities where they find people as sources of information, resources and recruits. More importantly, the people in these cities provide camouflage for terrorists and insurgents. The more disorder in these large cities, the better the opportunity for these threats to find sanctuary for their organizations. Even western technology has yet to develop the capability to detect such organizations out of the mass of people surrounding them. As America wages its war against terror, it is increasingly likely that we will find ourselves involved in either direct action within urban environments, or pre-emptive SASO activities in attempts to restore order and rid our enemies of their safe-havens.

At the higher end of the operational spectrum, it is just as likely that we will face an increased need to conduct urban operations. The Training and Doctrine Command (TRADOC) recently produced a white paper concerning the COE and states the following about urban operations:

> Opponents will attempt to offset air, intelligence, surveillance, and reconnaissance and other US technological advantages by fighting during periods of limited visibility and in complex terrain and urban environments where he can gain sanctuary from US effects, while denying these areas and their inherent protective characteristics to US forces. The use of complex and urban terrain, decentralized operations, and focused strikes combining fires and maneuver against key capabilities, will lead to more frequent engagements that develop more rapidly, require rapid change in organization, and consume manpower and resources. Loss of contact will have greater consequences than in more open environments against more predictable echeloned forces. Lines of communications and operations will be difficult to secure in a continuous basis. These measures will also reduce engagement ranges of weapon and acquisition systems, degrading US advantages with respect to standoff engagement.[9]

In short, our enemies have learned that to fight us in open terrain with conventional forces will result in certain defeat for them. They would be fighting where we have all of the advantages. Instead, contemporary adversaries will seek to balance the playing field by forcing us to prosecute urban operations where our weapons' range, acquisition, intelligence and

---

[9] TRADOC White Paper, "The Future Operational Environment," 4 May 2001.

firepower systems' advantages are reduced if not negated. The Chechens learned this same lesson while fighting against the Russians. Chechen fighters felt comfortable fighting in the cities and mountains, but in the plains in between, they were decimated by Russian firepower.[10]

Some argue that because the enemy has chosen to fight in the cities, this does not mean we must follow them there and fight. But we may not have the luxury of avoiding such urban fights. This is particularly true should the enemy occupy and develop urban strongpoints astride key avenues of approach or lines of communication. Korea offers a perfect example of this exact dilemma. The Korean terrain is very restrictive with its mobility corridors along narrow river valleys bordered by steep mountain ridges. The channeling affect of this terrain demands that heavy ground forces restrict their maneuver along narrow corridors in the valley floors that are increasingly urban. Should enemy forces occupy urban strongpoints along these axes, U.S. forces would have no choice but to clear the enemy from them as they attempt to maneuver either forward or backwards. This is particularly true for legacy forces and will remain so, until a force is fielded capable of bypassing such urban areas using vertical envelopment for example.

Even if we are capable of bypassing such enemy strongpoints, there still remains a requirement to contain bypassed enemy forces to prevent them from striking out of their urban complexes once bypassed. The Russians learned this lesson in their first incursion into Chechnya in 1994, and are still struggling to overcome the challenge of protecting lines of communications from bypassed enemy in urban strongpoints. Once again, we too will struggle with this challenge while still operating with legacy and interim equipped forces.

As the Army continues to become an increasingly strategic, CONUS-based force and less forward deployed, it must deploy into theaters of crisis using aerial ports of debarkation (APODs) and seaports of debarkations (SPODs) for the foreseeable future. These APODs and SPODs are typically surrounded by or adjacent to urban areas. Analysis of the COE finds that

---

[10] Sean J.A. Edwards, *Mars Unmasked: The Changing Face of Urban Operations*, (Santa Monica,

America's enemies have learned the dangers of letting the US forces build combat power unchallenged in the theater of operations.

> In addition to efforts designed to preclude US involvement, potential adversaries also recognize the need to develop a capability to operationally exclude US forces, should their commitment become inevitable. Operational exclusion is aimed at preventing US forces from obtaining and using operational bases in the region. This approach is designed to attack expected historical patterns of US deployment and employment. This US pattern is seen as an operational paradigm and structure that requires entry operations, force build up and air and missile campaign prior to any full dimensional operation. [11]

Until such time as US forces possess a strategic airlift and sealift capability that does not require the use of existing APODs and SPODs, they will be required to clear the surrounding urban areas. For a recent example of this exact challenge, one needs to look no further than Camp Rhino located in the vicinity of Kandahar, Afghanistan. This operational base is located on an airfield surrounded by urban complexes, and has required ground and aviation forces to conduct clearing operations on several occasions.

Summary

There has always been a serious requirement to conduct urban operations. For example, in 1985, approximately 15% of the Federal Republic of Germany was urbanized.[12] For the average NATO brigade commander that would have meant about 25 towns and villages in his 12 by 25 kilometer sector.[13] The opposing division commander engaged in concentrating for a breakthrough would have faced a mirror image of the above density. At any one time he would have had to deal with ten to fifteen towns and villages – his division's frontage varying between 8 to 12 kilometers.[14] But the very nature of the cold war, which was successful by its deterrence, prevented the U.S. from ever having to face the reality of fighting such urban engagements.

CA: RAND Arroyo Center, 2000), 28.

[11] TRADOC White Paper, "The Future Operational Environment."

[12] Col. Trevor N. Dupuy, USA (Ret.) and Col. Franklin D. Margiotta, USAF (Ret.), eds. *International Military and Defense Encyclopedia* (Washington, New York: Brassey's (US) Inc., 1993), s.v. "Urban Warfare" by Lutz Unterseher.

[13] Ibid.

[14] Ibid.

The nature of the post-cold war era has forced America to face up to the realities of fighting in the urban environment. Notwithstanding, as evidence that urban operations already are increasing in occurrence, U.S. forces have been committed 27 times since 1977. Ten of those missions took place in urban areas, while 11 others were conducted in combined urban and rural environments.[15] The U.S. is not alone in experiencing growing involvement in urban operations. The Russians with their experience in Grozny I and II have also begun to shift greater emphasis towards urban operations. The Russians latest doctrine, *Combat in Cities* states, "The built-up area is unavoidable due to the extent of urbanization."[16]

It is not enough to speak of preparing for "future urban operations." The future is here today and requiring preparation to engage in urban operations even as the U.S. Army moves toward the objective force. Preparation requires solid doctrine, realistic training programs and facilities, and appropriate equipment to ensure success on the urban battlefield when the time comes to fight there.

---

[15] Susan Villella, "Urban Evasion – A Necessary Component of Urban Operations," JSSA SERE Newsletter, October 1998, *http://www.geocities.com/Pentagon/6453/urbanevasion.html*, 2/23/02.

[16] Capt. Kevin W. Brown, "The Urban Warfare Dilemma – U.S. Casualties vs. Collateral Damage," *Marine Corps Gazette* 81, no. 1 (January 1997): 38.

CHAPTER 3

CONTEMPORARY URBAN LESSONS: MOGADISHU AND GROZNY I

"The practical value of history is to throw the film of the past through the
material projector of the present onto the screen of the future."

B.H. Liddell Hart

Introduction

No two operations display the dynamics of the contemporary urban operating
environment more than the experiences of the U.S. Task Force Ranger in Mogadishu and the
Russian Federation Forces in Grozny I. For this reason, these two operations are examined with
the purpose of addressing the challenges of such urban operations and to analyze the lessons
gleaned from them. The purpose of this section is not to conduct a history lesson, but an attempt
to gain a better understanding of the contemporary, urban operations environment we currently
face.

Mogadishu, Somalia

Background

In the summer of 1993, as UN peacekeeping forces were attempting to perform their
UNOSOM II mission, they began to encounter confrontations with the Somali National Alliance
(SNA) and its warlord clan leader, Mohammed Farah Aidid. Aidid, one of the most powerful
warlord clan leaders also possessed the most heavily armed militia in the Mogadishu. Aidid's
forces used guerilla tactics, which included low-level attacks at weaker UN targets, in order to
avoid direct confrontations with UNISOM forces.[17] Their favorite tactic was the ambush, which
avoided fixed fights and was conducted only when his forces possessed an advantage.[18] These
confrontations between the UN forces and Aidid continued to escalate, culminating when Aidid's
SNA militia ambushed a Pakistani UN force conducting a mission to shut down Aidid's pirate

---

[17] Edwards, *Mars Unmasked: The Changing Face of Urban Operations*, 12.
[18] Ibid.

radio station.[19] After this ambush which killed twenty-four and wounding fifty more, Aidid went into hiding and remained at large, while his SNA continued to attack UN forces.[20]

In response to this massacre of UN forces, the UN security counsel with sponsorship from the US authorized action against those responsible. UN resolution 837 empowered UNISOM II to arrest and detain those responsible for the massacre for "prosecution, trial, and punishment" and to use all necessary measures to establish UN authority throughout Somalia.[21]

After UNISOM II's initial operations and skirmishes against Aidid, the SNA countered with a series of mortar attacks on the American QRF heliport at Mogadishu airfield. Following the mortar attacks, the US established Task Force Ranger (TFR) which consisted of a Delta detachment, members of the 75th Ranger Regiment, and air support from elements of the Task Force 160 using MH-60 Blackhawks and AH-6J Littlebirds. As the operation progressed, the SNA continued to conduct mortar attacks on the airfield and even shot down a US MH-60 using rocket propelled grenades (RPG-7.)[22] As a result of this escalation, the US forces requested the support of armor, but were turned down by the Secretary of Defense for fear of escalating the conflict.[23] In the meantime, TFR continued to conduct raid missions by both ground and air against the SNA capturing either Aidid's lieutenants or attempting to capture Aidid himself.

It is on this backdrop that the events of the TFR raid occurred in the afternoon of 3 October 1993. What was planned to be a rapidly executed raid quickly turned into an eighteen-hour firefight. TFR consisted of an assault force of 75 Rangers, 40 Delta Force troops and 17 helicopters.[24] The light infantry were armed with small arms, the relieving convoy had nothing heavier than .50 caliber machineguns, and close air support consisted of MH-60 Blackhawks and

---

[19] Ibid.
[20] Ibid.
[21] Kenneth Allard, *Somolia Operations: Lessons Learned*, (Washington, D.C.: Defense University Press), 3.
[22] Major Clifford E. Day, "Critical Analysis on the Defeat of Task Force Ranger", (M.S. diss., US Army War College, March 1997), 6.
[23] Col (Ret) David Hackworth, *Hazardous Duty*, (New York, NY: Avon Books, 1996), 159.
[24] Edwards, *Mars Unmasked: The Changing Face of Urban Operations*, 13.

AH-6J Littlebirds.[25] The Somalis were armed only with small arms, RPGs and .51 caliber machine guns.

At approximately 1500, the key members of the SNA were scheduled to conduct a meeting in the Bakara Market area of Mogadishu. At 1540 TFR aboard helicopters inserted into the target area by fast roping the Rangers to isolate the target buildings on the ground.[26] Once the Rangers secured the outer cordon, the Delta commandos inserted aboard Littlebirds and conducted the penetration of the target building and seized the twenty-four SNA members. At the same time the TFR helicopters left the airfield base camp, the Rangers also deployed a ground convoy consisting of highly mobile multi-wheeled vehicles (HMMWV) and 5-ton trucks. The ground convoy was to link up with TFR at the objective in the Bakara Market area and extricate the TFR elements and the prisoners by ground.

All went basically according to plan until TFR began a withdrawal from the area. At that point, they came under heavy fire from small arms and RPGs, which knocked out several vehicles and one of the MH-60s hovering overhead. Elements of TFR were able to secure the helicopter crash site, but came under increasing fire and were immediately surrounded by a mob of SNA militia forces intermixed with women and children. The ground convoy of TFR attempted to reach the crash site, but due to intense RPG and small arms fire and its inability to locate the crash site, they were ordered back to the airfield.

At 1629, a second MH-60 was shot down by RPG fire and crashed about two miles from the initial raid site.[27] In response, TFR headquarters launched a rescue force comprised of 22 lightly armored vehicles, TFR soldiers, and a light infantry company from the 10th Mountain Division.[28] At approximately 1745, the rescue force attacked into Mogadishu, but was stopped by

---

[25] Day, "Critical Analysis On the Defeat of Task Force Ranger", 21.
[26] Day, "Critical Analysis on the Defeat of Task Force Ranger", 7.
[27] Col Daniel P. Bolger, *Death Ground: Today's American Infantry in Combat*, (Novato, CA: Presidio Press, 1999), 203.
[28] Day, "Critical Analysis on the Defeat of Task Force Ranger", 9.

blockades and intense RPG and small arms fire.[29] An hour later, after firing almost 60,000 rounds against the enemy, the rescue force broke contact and withdrew back to the airfield base camp.[30]

At 2320, a UN force of four Pakistani tanks, twenty-four Malaysian armored personnel carriers (APC), about fifty soldiers from TFR, and two light infantry companies of the 10th Mountain Division attacked towards the Bakara Market to link up with the surrounded elements of TFR.[31] Advancing by fire and maneuver against determined militia resistance, it took the rescue force nearly two and half hours to reach the cutoff TFR elements. It was not until 0530 the next morning that the rescue column and TFR elements reached the safety of the Pakistani base camp.[32]

Although the mission of capturing SNA leadership was accomplished, the US forces suffered 18 killed and seventy-four wounded.[33] The equipment loss totaled two MH-60 helicopters destroyed and four severely damaged as well as several vehicles either destroyed or damaged. The Somalis suffered some 500 killed and at least a thousand were hospitalized.[34] While technically a success, the overall mission was a hollow victory and could be better described as a strategic failure for the US, which eventually led to an expedited withdrawal of US forces from Somalia.

Lessons Learned

Several factors contributed to Aidid's and the SNA's success against TFR. First, fighting in an urban environment inhibited many of the U.S. advantages, particularly situational awareness and firepower. This lack of situational awareness created difficulty for the TFR ground convoy and rescue columns to navigate through the myriad of streets, although they possessed state of the

---

[29] Ibid.
[30] Ibid.
[31] Ibid., 10.
[32] Ibid., 39.
[33] Edwards, *Mars Unmasked: The Changing Face of Urban Operations*, 35.
[34] Ibid.

art overhead imagery support. The urban environment also eroded much of the U.S. forces standoff capability and limited the fighting to close in, small arms engagements.

The SNA's use of RPGs was especially effective against the U.S. forces. Besides bringing down two MH-60 Blackhawks, the RPG gave the SNA a firepower advantage in the close fight over the U.S. forces. This is particularly so in light of claims that the TFR elements were not equipped with M-203 or MK-19 support during the conduct of the raid. Compounding this lack of firepower on the ground, the raid was not supported by AC-130 gunships that normally fly in support of the Rangers. Instead the mission had to rely on attack aviation helicopter assets for indirect fire support, thus further exposing them to the risk of being shot down by RPGs.

The raid's lack of combined arms was particularly acute, especially when they encountered enemy roadblocks. Major General Garrison's task force never envisioned armor as part of its force package.[35] Its tactics were to strike with surprise and speed, and up until October 3, those tactics had worked.[36] As a result the thin-skinned convoy of TFR sustained a 50% casualty rate as it exfiltrated the city.[37] After 10th Mountain failed in its attempts to reenter the city, it took an ad hoc Malaysian, Pakistani, and U.S. combined arms team to finally break through and relieve the pinned Rangers.

The local population support given to the SNA militia also caused many dilemmas for U.S. soldiers. Using the U.S. forces own rules of engagement (ROE) against them, Somali fighters hid behind unarmed civilians or used them to point out TFR positions so they could engage the Rangers. These tactics initially caused U.S. forces to hold their fire and restricted their use of airpower support, thus giving the SNA militia an advantage. Eventually, the U.S. forces were forced to change their application of ROE to survive this fight, but still could not

---

[35] Mark Bowden, *Black Hawk Down: A Story of Modern War,* (New York: Penguin Books, 1999,2000), 340.
[36] Ibid.

employ airpower beyond attack aviation support due to the high concentration of civilian populace.

Some of the combat lessons learned by the U.S. forces in Mogadishu are best summarized by important training the Rangers now stress called the four fundamentals; marksmanship, physical fitness, battle drills, and medical training.[38] From their experiences in Mogadishu, the Rangers believe that to be successful in urban combat, a unit must have mastered these four basic areas. As a result, they have re-examined their marksmanship program, still emphasizing the basics while expanding it to include close quarters combat marksmanship. To overcome the physical and mental challenges of urban combat, they now conduct physical fitness training that is combat focused. The typical medic to soldier ratio in units is 1 medic to every 48 soldiers.[39] The Rangers now attempt to qualify everyone as a combat lifesaver, and have maintained a 90% currency rate in efforts to overcome the low number of assigned medics.[40]

Another important lesson is that moving and fighting in urban terrain requires 360 degree security/awareness and judicious use of cover. The Rangers found that stacking and moving along walls was extremely perilous. Additionally, things can and will go wrong, such as communications failures, ammunition and water consumption, and personnel accountability. This requires planning of contingencies for day and night operations along with each critical vulnerability that develops during mission analysis. The Rangers participating in the raid on October 3 were under the impression that it was going to be another "in-and-out" mission. They took only one canteen of water, their basic load of ammunition, and did not take night vision

---

[37] Ibid., 341.
[38] CSM Michael Hall and SFC Micheal T. Kennedy, "The Urban Area During Support Missions Case Study: Mogadishu," in *Capital Preservation: Preparing for Urban Operations in the Twenty-First Century*, ed. Russell W. Glenn (Santa Monica: Rand, 2001), 546.
[39] Ibid., 549.
[40] Ibid.

devices.[41] As the mission extended into the unforeseen night, the lack of night vision, low water availability, and heavy ammunition and medical supply expenditure became critical.

Mogadishu also reinforced the principle of maintaining a ground-based reserve, particularly in the manpower-intensive urban environment. After the SNA shot down two helicopters, there was no uncommitted ground-based reserve available to enable the U.S. forces to regain the initiative and momentum. This lesson is particularly important in light of the argument that the only urban operation the U.S. forces undertake should consist of raids and missions at the lower end of the operational spectrum. When the raid failed to achieve surprise and was pinned down, it was a conventional, combined-arms, ground-based force conducting house-to-house fighting that was required to rescue TFR.

Grozny I, Chechnya

Background

The Russian Federation Forces first battle for control of Grozny, Chechnya occurred a little over a year after the U.S. battle in Mogadishu. The battles for Grozny and those that occurred in the area and villages surrounding Grozny covered the entire spectrum of operations. For the purpose of this monograph we will examine the first battle for Grozny, which typifies what is considered high-intensity urban operations.

Chechnya was important to Russia for several reasons, but primarily because of its relationship to the oil reserves and transportation networks in the region. Major Russian oil pipelines run from the Caspian basin through Chechnya and the Transcaucasus to the Black Sea.[42] Chechnya also possesses roads and rail networks that are important to accessing the oil reserves in the Caspian basin. Russia was further concerned that by allowing the Chechens to break free from the Federation, other Republics in the region would try to do the same.

---

[41] Bowden, *Black Hawk Down: A Story of Modern War*, 215, 230.
[42] Edwards, *Mars Unmasked: The Changing Face of Urban Operations*, 23.

18

In October 1991 President Jokar Dudayev, a former Soviet Air Force general, declared Chechnya's independence from the Soviet Union.[43] The Ingush, the second most populous nationality in Chechnya, opposed Dudayev and allied themselves with the Russian Federation.[44] In November of 1994, the Ingush resistance with the support of Russian aircraft and advisors attacked Grozny but were repulsed by Chechen forces loyal to Dudayev. Russia denied involvement in this attack initially, but after Dudayev paraded captured Russian soldiers before TV cameras, they finally admitted their complicity in supporting the Ingush.[45]

On December 11, 1994 Yeltsin ordered the Russian Army to invade Chechnya, establish a peacekeeping mission between the Chechens and the Ingush in order to eventually assimilate Chechnya back into the federation. Russian forces consisting of about 23,800 men, 80 tanks, 208 APC/IFV's, and 182 artillery pieces invaded Chechnya along 3 axis of advance.[46]

The Chechens started the war with an estimated 15,000 men, 35-50 tanks (most believed to be inoperable), 40 IFVs, 109 artillery pieces, multiple rocket launchers, mortars and approximately 150 anti-aircraft weapons.[47] They also had a large number of RPGs at their disposal. It is unclear how many forces actually defended Grozny since the number varies from source to source. Estimates put their strength somewhere around 1,000 at the lower end and up to 10,000 at the higher end.[48] What is known is that the Chechen's defended Grozny with two battle-hardened battalions, the Abkhazian and the Muslim along with a special brigade.[49] These forces often fought in elements of up to 200 men, arriving to the scene of battle in privately

---

[43] Timothy L. Thomas, "The Battle of Grozny: Deadly Classroom for Urban Combat," *Parameters*, (Summer 1999): 87.

[44] Captain Chad Rupe, "The Battle of Grozny: Lessons for Military Operations on Urbanized Terrain," *Armor*, no. 3 (May-June 1999): 20.

[45] Thomas, "The Battle of Grozny: Deadly Classroom for Urban Combat," 88.

[46] Ibid.

[47] Ibid.

[48] Olga Oliker, *Russia's Chechen Wars, 1994-2000: Lessons from Urban Combat*, (Santa Monica, CA: RAND, 2001), 13.

[49] Rupe, "The Battle of Grozny: Lessons for Military Operations on Urbanized Terrain," 20.

owned vehicles.[50] The more common organization, however, were three- or five-man cells consisting of a machine-gunner, an ammo bearer, an RPG-7 or -18, and a sniper. Five of these cells were normally linked into 15- to 25-man groups that fought together.[51] Three of these 25-man groups made up a 75-man unit responsible for fighting within a designated quadrant.[52]

Grozny was a city of nearly 490,000 residents and included many multiple story buildings and industrial installations, and covered some 100 square miles.[53] Within Grozny, the Chechens defended the city using three defensive lines concentrically around the Presidential Palace. The inner defense ring had a radius of 1.5 km, the middle was 2 to 5 km, and the outermost ring extended to the cities outskirts.[54] The Chechens established strongpoint defensive positions along the outer and middle rings, and prepared positions for tank and artillery in the inner defense. Similar to the SNA militia encountered by the U.S. in Somalia, they used the swarm technique of fighting, or as they put it, they let the situation do the organizing.

On New Year's Eve, the Russians' northern force advanced on Grozny with about 6,000 men. The Northern Force consisted of the 131st "Maikop" Motorized Rifle Brigade, the 81st Motorized Rifle Regiment, and the 20th Motorized Rifle Regiment.[55] Their plan was to attack Grozny in armored columns from the march without dismounting to clear buildings methodically along the way.[56] Instead, they would quickly seize important Chechen nodes such as the presidential palace, the railroad station, and government radio and television station buildings.[57] In the East, Russian Airborne forces seized the suburbs and railroad stations in support of the

---

[50] Thomas, "The Battle of Grozny: Deadly Classroom for Urban Combat," 96.
[51] Ibid.
[52] Oliker, *Russia's Chechen Wars, 1994-2000: Lessons from Urban Combat*, 19.
[53] Thomas, "The Battle of Grozny: Deadly Classroom for Urban Combat," 88.
[54] Rupe, "The Battle of Grozny: Lessons for Military Operations on Urbanized Terrain," 20.
[55] Thomas, "The Battle of Grozny: Deadly Classroom for Urban Combat," 88.
[56] Rupe, "The Battle of Grozny: Lessons for Military Operations on Urbanized Terrain," 20.
[57] Edwards, *Mars Unmasked: The Changing Face of Urban Operations*, 24.

Northern force. The forces in the West never advanced on Grozny, because Chechen civilians impeded their advance.[58]

As the northern columns advanced, the Russian soldiers expected to disband poorly trained civilian mobs by demonstrating a mere show of force.[59] Many of the drivers, dismounts and leaders had been drawn from separate forces throughout the Russian Army and hurriedly thrown together for this operation.[60] According to eyewitness accounts, many of the soldiers in this non-cohesive unit were impaired by consumption of Vodka and asleep in the back of the infantry IFVs.[61] Very few IFVs even had a full complement of dismounts. Further complicating the operation, vehicle commanders did not possess maps of the city and resorted to merely following the vehicles in front of them.[62] As a result, these columns became lost and rather than advancing rapidly on the Presidential Palace, stumbled into a series of well-planned Chechen ambushes.

The Chechen ambushes destroyed the lead and trail vehicles in the Russian armored columns successfully bottling the remainder of the vehicles into narrow streets that became kill zones. Untrained Russian soldiers remained in their vehicles and offered little to no resistance, believing that they were safer inside their vehicles than outside fighting. This allowed Chechen anti-armor forces to systematically destroy the Russian armored vehicles using either Molotov cocktails thrown from rooftops or RPGs fired from basements or upper floors of the surrounding buildings. Russian tank guns proved ineffective since they could neither depress low enough nor elevate high enough to engage Chechens in the basements, higher floors or rooftops. In some

---

[58] Rupe, "The Battle of Grozny: Lessons for Military Operations on Urbanized Terrain," 21.
[59] Ibid.
[60] Oliker, *Russia's Chechen Wars, 1994-2000: Lessons from Urban Combat*, 11.
[61] Rupe, "The Battle of Grozny: Lessons for Military Operations on Urbanized Terrain," 21.
[62] Oliker, *Russia's Chechen Wars, 1994-2000: Lessons from Urban Combat*, 11.

instances where soldiers did dismount, the Chechens had barricaded the first floor windows of the surrounding buildings leaving the Russian dismounts to fight and die in the open streets.[63]

The first unit to penetrate into Grozny's center, the 1st Battalion of the 131st "Maikop" Brigade, fell short of the Presidential Palace. By January 3, 1995 it had lost almost 800 of its 1,000 men, 20 of 26 tanks, and 102 of its 120 armored vehicles.[64]   After the devastating losses of January 1-3, the Russians regrouped and adjusted their tactics. They began to fight with combined arms teams using infantry dismounts to clear buildings, supported by teams of two IFVs and a tank.[65] They also used massive amounts of indirect fire. According to some accounts for a period of 20 days, Russian artillery rained down on the town at a rate of up to 4,000 rounds a minute.[66]

By January 10 the Russians had created two corridors into the city to resupply stranded units, and evacuate casualties. It was not until the 19th that they gained control of the Presidential Palace but only after bombing it from the air, which forced the Chechens to withdraw. It took the Russians through most of January to seal off Grozny from Chechen reinforcements, and until the end of February to finally gain control of the city of Grozny.[67]

At the end of this first fight for Grozny, the Russian losses were estimated to be 1,500 dead, 6,000 wounded with almost 300 armored vehicles lost.[68] The Chechen losses, although hard to confirm, are estimated at 3,300–6,700 killed and untold number of wounded.[69] An estimated 25,000 non-combatants also lost their lives.[70]

---

[63] Arthur L. Speyer, III, The Two Sides of Grozny," in *Capital Preservation: Preparing for Urban Operations in the Twenty-First Century*, ed. Russell W. Glenn (Santa Monica: Rand, 2001), 70.
[64] Ibid.
[65] Rupe, "The Battle of Grozny: Lessons for Military Operations on Urbanized Terrain," 20.
[66] Thomas, "The Battle of Grozny: Deadly Classroom for Urban Combat," 88.
[67] Edwards, *Mars Unmasked: The Changing Face of Urban Operations*, 26.
[68] Ibid., 35.
[69] Ibid.

Lessons Learned

An analysis of the Russian's first Grozny campaign yields numerous lessons for contemporary urban operations. After their initial failures, the Russians relooked their urban tactics by drawing upon lessons they learned in WWII; particularly from their fighting in Berlin.[71] As a result they reverted back to the execution of firepower intensive attrition operations and away from their initial maneuver based operations. Rather than conducting rapid maneuver through the city in an effort to seize "key nodes", they began to methodically clear buildings block by block using heavy amounts of firepower.

They relearned how to clear multi-story buildings and then defend them from Chechen counterattack. They made greater use of combined arms using dismounted forces to lead and clear while armor / mechanized assets and snipers provided overwatch. Additionally they used smoke to screen their movement in the open and employed demolitions to facilitate movement within buildings. Artillery was used to provide both indirect and direct fire support for the clearing teams.

Grozny brought the significance of training for urban operations to the forefront. Urban operations are not simply a modified version of warfare in open terrain. Although many of the principles remain the same, urban warfare with its three dimensional nature and civilian population, is unique and distinct from all other environments. For this reason, armed forces must train to fight in this environment if they are to be successful. The Russian force that entered Grozny had not trained for UO and the results were catastrophic. One Russian officer was quoted as stating that the Russian Army had not rehearsed an assault on a built up area for 20 to 25 years.[72] The Russian *Spetsnaz*[73] had indeed trained for urban operations, but only at the small-

---

[70] Ibid.
[71] Oliker, *Russia's Chechen Wars, 1994-2000: Lessons from Urban Combat*, 23.
[72] Thomas, "The Battle of Grozny: Deadly Classroom for Urban Combat," 89.
[73] Russian Special Forces.

23

scale, counter-terrorist level, not high intensity urban warfare.[74] The motorized, conventional forces that entered Grozny were woefully under-prepared. Only five to six hours of the year's mandated 151 total hours of squad, platoon, and company tactical training had been dedicated to the urban environment.[75]

Employing the right equipment properly in urban operations was another lesson. While Grozny I caused some to conclude that tanks were not suited for fighting in cities, the Russians sought tactics to employ them more effectively. For instance they began using them in combined arms teams as well as devising rudimentary wire mesh screens around the tanks to cause early detonation of incoming shaped charges fired against exposed vehicles.[76]

The Russians came to believe that the Infantry needed the same capabilities in the direct fire, hand-held mode as could be provided by both artillery and tanks. This became especially relevant when one or both of these assets could not provide support due to obstacles. They also began to employ the thermobaric weapon, the RPO-A Schmel, as "pocket artillery".[77] Finally units were equipped with special devices such as lightweight ladders, grappling hooks, secure / tactical communications at the lowest levels, and remotely piloted vehicles (RPVs).

Summary

In examining these two contemporary urban operations, that cover the spectrum of operations, several common themes become apparent. First, both the U.S. and Russian forces initially attempted maneuver operations against an opponent who they possessed a poor intelligence assessment of and ultimately underestimated. This underestimation allowed the U.S. and the Russians to be surprised by an unsophisticated enemy, armed with a healthy supply of RPG's, and who were not afraid to fight. Second, both forces initially failed to conduct their urban operations with a fully integrated combined arms team, much less a joint effort. And

---

[74] Oliker, *Russia's Chechen Wars, 1994-2000: Lessons from Urban Combat*, 8.
[75] Ibid.
[76] Ibid., 25.

finally both forces had to cope with the additional challenges and dilemmas posed by the presence of civilians on the battlefield in the urban environment. To overcome their initial failings, both the U.S. and Russian forces changed their operational approach from one of maneuver to one of heavy firepower in an attrition style operation. In addition, after sustaining casualties and loss of friendly lives, both forces eventually adopted improved, combined arms tactics, while at the same time resorting to the killing of civilians and the infliction of greater collateral damage.

These two vignettes provide a brief look at the nature of the contemporary UO environment. Furthermore, they offer what is representative of future urban warfare and the lessons they provide should be used to develop how the Army prepares for urban operations. These vignettes should lead one to ask whether or not the U.S. Army is adequately prepared to fight in the contemporary urban environment. Do our urban operation's doctrine, training and resourcing programs address the challenges faced by the forces involved in these two operations? And finally, how feasible are emerging doctrinal concepts such as nodal attack in an environment like those of Mogadishu and Grozny? In the next chapter the author will attempt to answer some of these questions by first looking at the state of the Army's UO doctrine.

---

[77] Ibid., 26.

CHAPTER 4

URBAN OPERATIONS DOCTRINE

> Each urban operation will be distinct from any other….Therefore, there will always exist an innate tension between Army doctrine, the actual context of the urban operation, and future realities.
>
> FM 3-06, Urban Operations

Introduction

Doctrine is the cornerstone for how the U.S. Army fights. It provides the military organization with a common philosophy, a language, a purpose, and a unity of effort.[78] It establishes the fundamental principles that guide military actions, provides a common perspective from which U.S. forces can plan and operate and ultimately influences the way forces train, equip, and organize. Without doctrine providing a beacon, these activities would not be synchronized, but would occur in an ad hoc manner.[79] Training particularly relies on doctrine for uniform standards and consistency in an organization's methods. Furthermore, the new FM 3-0 concept of strategic responsiveness means units must get training right before being alerted, not after.[80]

To remain relevant, doctrine must be continually re-evaluated and improved, especially in an era of rapidly changing operational environments and evolving technology. Over the last decade, this re-evaluation of our UO doctrine has been slow to evolve despite numerous calls for its improvement from both within and outside of DOD. In the past two years however, the realization that cities are important in the COE has caused a flurry of activity to improve our UO capabilities, particularly in the doctrine arena. Because of the importance of doctrine to the entire

---

[78] U.S. Army, FM 3-06 *Urban Operations*, 2002, viii.

[79] Russel W. Glenn, *We Band of Brothers: A Call for Joint Operations Doctrine*, (Santa Monica, CA: Rand, 1999), 17.

[80] Ibid.

DOTMLF[81] process, this has been the initial focus of DOD in its attempts to transform our force's capabilities to conduct UO.

UO Doctrine Shortfalls

As early as 1994, the Defense Science Board concluded that UO would continue to be a major concern for U.S. forces and recommended that DOD take a systematic approach to improving urban warfighting capabilities including the establishment of joint doctrine.[82] The need for joint doctrine was further emphasized in a February 2000 GAO report, which found current Army and Marine Corps urban doctrine only focused on how their respective forces conducted UO rather than operations in which multiple services and allies operated with one another.[83] The report also stated that UO doctrine was oriented towards European cities, the focus of the Cold War, rather than the more primitive cities of developing nations. Finally, UO doctrine did not address the complexities and challenges of the modern urban battlespace such as the presence of civilians, shantytowns, and complex city infrastructure.

The following additional UO doctrinal shortfalls were also noted by numerous sources, namely the RAND Corporation's Arroyo Center:[84]

- UO doctrine lacked a combined arms focus
- Too focused on high-intensity UO; did not address the full spectrum
- Too tactically focused; did not cover the operational level
- Did not adequately describe the nature of urban areas
- Based on Cold War enemy threat, primarily Warsaw Pact forces
- Shortfalls in intelligence collection, analysis, and dissemination in the UO environment
- Lacked guidance for Command and Control; particularly in the joint and combined environment
- Limited reference to non-combatant considerations
- Did not describe weapons effects beyond infantry weapons
- Possessed limited training beyond infantry battle drills

---

[81] Doctrine, Organization, Training, Materiel, Leadership, People, Facilities
[82] Defense Science Board, *Report of the Defense Science Board Task Force on Military Operations in Built-Up Areas (MOBA)*, (Washington, D.C.: Office of the Under Secretary of Defense for Acquisition and Technology, 1994), 57.
[83] GAO, *Military Capabilities: Focused Attention Needed to Prepare U.S. Forces for Combat in Urban Areas*: 8.
[84] Russell W. Glenn, *Denying the Widow-Maker: Summary of Proceedings RAND-DBBL Conference on Military Operation s on Urbanized Terrain*, (Santa Monica, CA: RAND, 1998), 12-14.

Based on these negative assessments of the Armed Forces UO doctrine, it was evident that our doctrine needed to be updated and in some cases new concepts developed.

Joint UO Doctrine

Joint doctrine provides military officers who will lead joint military operations, guidance for conducting joint and combined activities across the broad spectrum of military operations. Lessons from Mogadishu and Grozny displayed the importance and necessity of conducting joint operations when fighting in cities, yet as late as 2000 our forces still possessed no written doctrine for joint UO.

To rectify the lack of joint UO doctrine, the Office of the Secretary of Defense (OSD) for Policy established an informal urban working group to develop this much needed joint doctrine as well as develop a master plan for the coordination of all of the services UO development.[85] In addition, the Joint Staff (J8) now chairs a general officer-level Special Studies Group to advise the Secretary of Defense regarding the establishment of a DOD Executive Agent and the development of a DOD Master Plan to address urban capabilities.[86]

In September 1999, the Joint Urban Working Group obtained agreement from the services for an initial concept for conducting urban operations jointly in urban settings.[87] The Marine Corps was assigned the responsibility of producing a joint publication (JP 3-06) that integrates current service efforts to develop doctrine and defines terminology for joint urban operations.[88] JP 3-06, expected to be published in June 2001, is still in its final coordinating draft phase, with a new expected publication date of June 2002. In the interim the Air Force has

---

[85] Joint Advanced Warfighting Program. "Draft DOD Roadmap for Improving Capabilities for Urban Operations", 20 November 2001, 5.

[86] Ibid, 5.

[87] GAO, *Military Capabilities: Focused Attention Needed to Prepare U.S. Forces for Combat in Urban Areas,* 9.

[88] Ibid.

published a *Handbook for Joint Urban Operations*, providing the first joint UO doctrine for the U.S Armed Forces.[89]

Army UO Doctrine

In the past two years, the Army has made great strides forward in the development and re-writing of its UO doctrine. The new FM 3-0 Operations sets the tone for these operations in a clear break from the 1993 version of FM 100-5 Operations. Whereas previous doctrine stressed bypassing cities, which slowed maneuver forces' tempo, FM 3.0 states that cities are likely battlegrounds that will require full-spectrum dominance. It also recognizes that urban operations occur in an "environment" rather than merely "complex terrain" with man-made obstacles. They are unique operations that require detailed intelligence preparation of the battlefield (IPB), careful planning, and thorough preparation.[90] UO are further complicated by an intricate social structure of the population as well as the nature of three-dimensional topography.[91]

Previous Army doctrine was primarily based on two manuals, FM 90-10 *Military Operations on Urban Terrain*, dated August 1979 and FM 90-10-1 *An Infantryman's Guide to Combat in Built-Up Areas,* dated May 1993. This doctrine's focus was on the Air Land Battle, conventional Warsaw Pact threats, high-intensity combat, and phased operations.[92] In reviewing these manuals, the Army found that while many doctrinal principles were still valid, these documents fell short of what the Army needed in the contemporary urban environment.[93] For instance, FM 90-10 had not been updated since it was first published in August 1979, and FM 90-10-1, *An Infantryman's Guide to Combat in Built-Up Areas*, was exactly that; it was an

---

[89] U.S. Department of Defense, *Handbook for Joint Urban Operations*. (Washington, D.C.: U.S. Government Printing Office, 2000).

[90] U.S. Army, FM 3.0 *Operations*, Washington D.C.: Department of the Army, 2001, 6-76

[91] Ibid.

[92] Combined Arms MOUT Task Force, "Mission Need Statement For Urban Operations Training Capability." Annex A, 23 Feb 2001, 5-6.

[93] Mr. John Bastone, Combined Arms Task Force, phone interview with author on Feb. 5, 2002.

Infantryman's guide that lacked a broader combined arms perspective.[94] Other Army doctrinal

manuals provided little guidance for those seeking to prepare for UO.[95]

The new Army UO doctrine thoroughly addresses the doctrinal shortfalls possessed by

the previous versions of the Army's manuals and publications. FM 3-06 *Urban Operations* and

FM 3-06.11 *Combined Arms Operations in Urban Terrain* now provide the Army's capstone

doctrinal base for urban operations. Unlike in the past, this new doctrine is no longer solely

tactical in nature. FM 3-06, which replaces FM 90-10, focuses on the operational level of urban

operations, whereas FM 3-06.11 is a combined arms tactical guide that replaces FM 90-10-1.

In addition to covering joint and multi-national / coalition issues, the new doctrine is

deeply rooted in a combined arms approach to urban fighting across the full spectrum of

operations; offensive, defensive, stability and support.   While high-intensity combat is still

prevalent throughout, these manuals also outline operations at the lower end of the operational

spectrum. It addresses many of the contemporary urban challenges such as non-contiguous

battlefields, asymmetrical threats, non-lethal weapons effects, information operations, ROE

(collateral damage / non-combatants casualties), and transitions (stability and support operations

to combat operations and back).[96]

In addition to the two capstone UO manuals, a comprehensive effort has been ongoing

throughout the Army to update proponent manuals across TRADOC. Urban operations

appendices to FMs 3-21.30 (7-30), *The Infantry Brigade;* 3-21.20 (7-20), *The Infantry Battalion;*

and 3-21.10 (7-10), *The Infantry Rifle Company* have been approved by the United States Army

Infantry School (USAIS).[97] Other branches such as Armor, Aviation, and Engineers are also

---

[94] Russell W. Glenn, *Marching Under Darkening Skies: The American Military and the Impending Urban Operations Threat,*(Santa Monica, CA: RAND, 1998), 11.
[95] Ibid.
[96] Joint Advanced Warfighting Program. "Draft DOD Roadmap for Improving Capabilities for Urban Operations", 20 November 2001, 5.
[97] Combined Arm MOUT Task Force, "Mission Need Statement For Urban Operations Training Capability." Annex A, 23 Feb 2001, 5-6.

30

reworking their doctrinal manual base to nest with the new capstone manuals. Finally, to ensure that training and TTPs[98] are linked into the new UO doctrine, Mission Training Plans (MTP's) are being updated, thus ensuring the establishment of adequate training standards.[99]

Emerging Doctrinal Concepts

Joint Doctrine

Besides just updating current doctrinal concepts, DOD is attempting to develop new concepts for how we conduct UO. Traditional approaches to UO have been considered "attritionist" in their approach due largely to the difficulty in acquiring information in the urban environment.[100] Without information regarding the nature, positions, and movements of the enemy force, the friendly force commander must rely on approaches that are static(siege), indiscriminate(rubble-ization), or which trade casualties for information by sending ground-forces blindly forward to establish and maintain close contact with the enemy (frontal assault).[101]

The draft Joint Doctrine for Urban Operations utilizes the following operational framework: **Understand, Shape, Engage, Consolidate, and Transition (USECT)**.[102] In the past, urban operations have emphasized the **Engage** component due to the lack of information.[103] Emerging approaches intend to leverage the **Understand** and **Shape** components prior to engaging by utilizing precision effects from less vulnerable positions.[104] This new concept attempts to achieve a "maneuverist" approach to UO through superior information, shaping operations, and precision strike against enemy nodes (see figure 1).[105] The intent is to achieve a

---

[98] Techniques, Tactics, and Procedures

[99] Mr. John Bastone, Combined Arms MOUT Task Force, Phone interview with author on Feb.5, 2002.

[100] "A Concept for Future Military Operations on Urbanized Terrain," A-1.

[101] Joint Advanced Warfighting Program. "Draft DOD Roadmap for Improving Capabilities for Urban Operations", 20 November 2001, 5.

[102] U.S. Department of Defense, Joint Staff, "Doctrine for Joint Urban Operations." Joint Publication 3-06. Final Draft, 2002.

[103] Joint Advanced Warfighting Program. "Draft DOD Roadmap for Improving Capabilities for Urban Operations", 20 November 2001, 5-6.

[104] Ibid.

[105] Ibid.

more surgical approach than traditional methods with the prospect of significantly reducing both friendly and civilian casualties, as well as collateral damage.[106] The linchpin to this approach is the ability to collect superior information and intelligence thereby gaining a better understanding within the urban environment. This requires capabilities that we do not yet possess.

One of the challenges with emerging doctrine is the concept of isolating, conducting precision strike against, and seizure of enemy nodes. This concept briefs well, but as seen in Mogadishu and Grozny, the enemy in contemporary UO may not always possess critical nodes, or identifiable centers of gravity. In the two instances listed, the enemy conducted what could better be described as a swarm technique, and was virtually non-nodal.

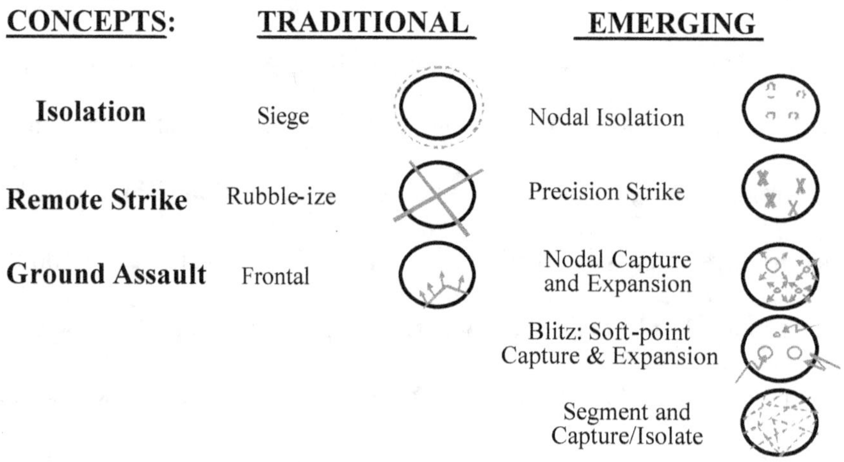

Figure 1. Emerging Joint UO Concepts

[107]

Joint experimentation must be conducted to validate these emerging doctrinal concepts. Such experimentation can determine the operational and technical requirements needed to successfully execute these future concepts. To achieve this, there must be a joint executive

---

[106] Ibid, 9

[107] Joint Advanced Warfighting Program. "Draft DOD Roadmap for Improving Capabilities for Urban Operations", 20 November 2001, 9.

agency to provide oversight, which the US Joint Forces Command (JFCOM) has been designated to provide. However, JFCOM is not planning to activate this agency until January 2003.[108]

Army UO Doctrine

The Army's emerging UO doctrinal concepts are very similar to those found in the JP 3-06. In particular the Army has also established a new operational framework with the following components: **Assess, Shape, Dominate, Transition (ASDT)**.[109] These four components provide a framework for viewing the application of Army combat power and capabilities within the urban environment.[110] The Army's UO framework varies from the Joint UO framework by substituting the Understand component with Assess, and the joint doctrine's Engage and Consolidate with Dominate. While the semantics vary somewhat between the two, they are virtually the same.

The new Army UO also uses the nodal concept, particularly in urban offensive operations. For instance the new doctrine states:

> In urban offensive operations, forces achieve dominance by successfully striking the enemy's center of gravity using multiple offensive actions from unexpected directions and throughout all dimensions. Army forces aim to dominate identifiable decisive points. Successful efforts against decisive points lead to effects on the center of gravity. [111]

The same challenges exist with this concept as mentioned with joint doctrine. Until our ISR capabilities are dramatically improved, its doubtful we will be able to conduct precision strike and dominant maneuver within cities, destroying the enemy's vulnerable nodes, thus causing his center of gravity to collapse.

Even if the nodes can be identified and isolated, at some point in the tactical level fight, ground forces will be required to conduct close quarters combat with enemy forces. For this

---

[108] Mr. John Bastone, Phone Interview, Feb.5, 2002.
[109] U.S. Army, FM 3-06 *Urban Operations*, Washington D.C.: Department of the Army, 2002, 5-1,5-2.

33

reason the Army's new doctrine appears to still bridge the gap between legacy force UO doctrine and future concepts as demonstrated in figures 2 and 3 listed below.[112]

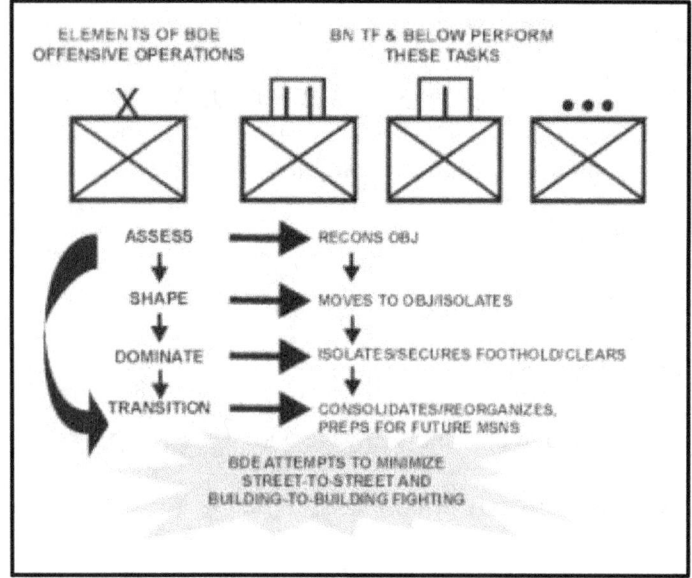

Figure 2. UO Offensive Framework   Figure 3. UO Defensive Framework

Summary

In summary, UO doctrine has undergone a long overdue re-write and is still being developed to make it relevant to the contemporary urban operating environment. At the Joint level there is an interim Joint UO document (T*he Handbook for Joint Urban Operations*) while JP 3-06 is being finalized. This new doctrine develops important future concepts in an attempt to solve UO dilemmas by significantly reducing both friendly and civilian casualties, as well as collateral damage. Many of the new joint doctrine concepts, such as nodal attack, still require further testing to ensure these concepts are valid as well as to develop services' contributions. This is an initiative that should be the first priority of the joint executive agency, which should be activated immediately, not a year from now.

---

[110] Ibid.

[111] Ibid, 5-6.

[112] U.S. Army, FM 3-06.11 *Combined Arms Operations In Urban Terrain*, Washington D.C.: Department of the Army, 2002, 4-16, 5-8.

Army service UO doctrine adequately addresses joint and coalition issues for urban operations and is nested with the emerging joint doctrine concepts. It has also advanced to cover the operational level of UO across the full spectrum with the development of FM 3-06 and continues to possess a strong tactical base through FM 3-06.11. Furthermore it is now a combined arms doctrine vice merely an infantryman-focused, tactical level doctrine.

What is required for current forces is a doctrine that will apply within the parameters of our current capabilities. Although the Army is moving towards urban operations that greater emphasize the assess and shape components, it realizes that our ISR capabilities are not yet fully developed. While Army UO doctrine possesses new operational framework concepts, it does still provide a bridge between the gap in our current legacy capabilities and future objective force capabilities that we wish to achieve.

Finally doctrine drives training…training supports doctrine. Our UO doctrinal foundation has been laid, and now the Army needs to begin to build the rest of the structure through training, organizing and equipping the force for fighting in the urban environment. But as we will see in the next chapter, where doctrine now leads, training has struggled to follow.

CHAPTER 5

URBAN OPERATIONS TRAINING

He who dies has lost. **In order to win, learn how to fight**; in battle, death sanctions every fault.

Jean Larteguy, *The Centurions*

Introduction

Even with the best doctrine, an army that is not trained or resourced properly will not be able to fight and win. Joint and service doctrine states that in order to be effective, military training should be based on pre-established, measurable standards, be realistic, challenging, and conducted as part of a joint and combined arms team.[113] Now that our UO doctrine has been improved, the next step is to ensure it is permeated throughout the services, and units in the field are trained to conduct UO jointly and as a combined arms team.

The Army is not prepared to fight in the urban environment without either sustaining heavy friendly casualties or causing excessive collateral damage and loss of civilian life, or both. This un-preparedness is due to the Army's lack of joint and combined arms training in the UO environment. These shortfalls are caused by insufficient training infrastructure, lack of command emphasis, insufficient time allocated for UO training, and improper techniques being trained.

Joint UO Training

Today, with a smaller armed force, fighting jointly for the U.S. is increasingly more important. Fighting joint is the way to leverage combat power with a smaller force, particularly when conducting UO operations that are traditionally manpower intensive. Furthermore, units should train how they fight, because experience teaches that in combat, they fight how they train. But is the Army training UO jointly? The results of this research determined that they are not.

---

[113] GAO, *Military Capabilities: Focused Attention Needed to Prepare U.S. Forces for Combat in Urban Areas*, 10.

Army units from company thru brigade level, when surveyed on how often their UO training incorporated other services responded unanimously with, "never."[114] Even when at the Combat Training Centers (CTCs), units did not conduct joint UO training.[115] Their lack of joint training was due primarily to limitations of the CTCs. In fact, the only CTC that offered such capability was the Joint Readiness Training Center (JRTC). The JRTC is considered joint because it offers some Air Force close air support (CAS) sorties during a unit's rotation. However, during the UO phase at JRTC, CAS sorties are not employed in the city due to the small size of the urban facilities.[116] Units typically employ organic attack aviation assets for such support.

The lack of joint training at the CTCs continues at home-station training. The home-station, joint UO training challenges are compounded by not only the lack of facilities, but also by the lack of exercise control infrastructure like that possessed by the CTCs. While it may not be feasible to overcome these home-station joint training shortfalls with live facilities, this is an area that could potentially be overcome through simulations (constructive and virtual facilities). However, units do not yet possess these capabilities.[117]

Combined Arms UO Training

Just as Mogadishu and Grozny displayed the importance of fighting as a joint force in the urban environment, they also demonstrated the importance of fighting as a combined arms team. The results of this research found that the Army, while getting better at training combined arms, still possesses some significant challenges before its UO training can be truly called combined arms.

---

[114] UO Survey results.
[115] Combat Training Centers include the National Training Center, Fort Irwin, CA. (trains primarily heavy forces); the Joint Readiness Training Center, Fort Polk, LA (trains primarily light forces); Combat Maneuver Training Center, Hohenfels, Germany (trains primarily European based heavy forces).
[116] Major Al Katz, JRTC LFX OIC, Phone interview with the author, 17 January 2002.
[117] CAMTF"Mission Need Statement For Urban Operations Training Capability," A-5,6.

The biggest shortfall in Army combined arms UO training appears to be cooperation between armor and dismounted infantry. According to light infantry units surveyed, when questioned how often they included armor support in their UO training, the unanimous answer was "never."[118] One of the reasons for this is the disparity between the location of its units and training resources. While armor and mechanized infantry units are best suited for combined arms training, such units typically do not possess adequate facilities for UO training at their home-station.[119] Light infantry units however, possess better urban training facilities, but do not have organic armor to facilitate combined arms UO training.[120]

When training at the CTCs, units are further hindered in conducting combined arms UO training. For example, the NTC until recently had no urban facility in which to conduct urban training. The CMTC, while possessing urban training facilities, until recently did not require units to conduct an urban scenario unless it was a training objective of the rotational unit.[121] At the JRTC, supporting heavy forces are staged at a separate intermediate staging base (ISB) than the light forces, and the first time they meet is on the battlefield after the scenario has started. While the units at JRTC do have the opportunity to conduct an urban mission during the rotation applying all combined arms, their lack of prior training prior to the rotations start proves to be a big detractor from unit success against the enemy.[122] Because of this lack of combined arms training, most leaders demonstrate a trend of limited understanding of basic UO doctrine and combined arms TTPs during their rotations.[123]

The survey did find some promising UO combined arms trends among the units surveyed. All units surveyed did employ organic fire support, engineer and attack aviation assets

---

[118] UO Survey results
[119] CAMTF "Mission Need Statement For Urban Operations Training Capability," A-5,6.
[120] GAO, *Military Capabilities: Focused Attention Needed to Prepare U.S. Forces for Combat in Urban Areas*, 11.
[121] Major Katz, JRTC MOUT OIC, interview with the author, 17 Jan 2002.
[122] Ibid.
[123] Ibid.

during their UO training.[124] While the fire support integration was often nothing more than inclusion of their fire support teams, there was a trend of incorporating fire support planning into units' UO training.[125] Engineers were incorporated into units' UO training as well, but suffered from the lack of real demolition breach opportunities and demolition effects simulators (DES).[126] Not surprising, units such as the 101st Airborne Division (Air Assault) responded with the greatest frequency for incorporating attack aviation into their UO training. However, all other units surveyed, also incorporated these assets into their training at least some of the time.[127] What this demonstrates is where units possess training facilities and are stationed together, they are conducting combined arms training.

To address the home station combined arms shortfall, the CAMTF master UO training strategy outlines a plan for the construction of urban training facilities, starting first at heavy unit posts.[128] This concept will allow light units to travel to heavy unit posts and conduct combined arms UO training. Moving light forces to train with heavy units is much easier and more cost effective than deploying heavy forces and their equipment to train at light infantry posts.[129]

As for the training centers, the NTC has begun the implementation of a new urban strategy, which includes the development of several UO sites to include one with 104 buildings.[130] The first units began use of completed portions of these facilities at the end of last year.[131] Furthermore, the CMTC is now incorporating UO scenarios into every rotation and adding additional urban structures each year.

The Army is still not training for urban warfare as a combined arms team. While there are several initiatives being developed and implemented to address this shortfall, they are not yet

---

[124] UO survey results
[125] Ibid.
[126] Ibid.
[127] Ibid.
[128] CAMTF"Mission Need Statement For Urban Operations Training Capability," A-5,6.
[129] Ibid.
[130] Concept Paper: NTC Urban Operations Training Requirements, 2 Oct 2000, 4.
[131] Ibid.

in place. In the meantime the Army must strive to train as a combined arms team at every opportunity, both at home-station and at the CTCs.

Full Spectrum Operations

Modern Army UO spans the full range of possible application of military power.[132] At the higher end of the spectrum of conflict is major theater of war dominated by offensive and defensive operations. At the lower or opposite end of the spectrum are urban peacetime military engagement (PME) activities. Between these two levels are smaller scale contingencies. Within these levels of intensity are four operational missions, offense, defense, stability and support.[133] In the COE, the Army must be prepared to conduct operations across the full spectrum of which most often will include operating in the urban environment in one fashion or another.

When units are conducting urban training, survey results indicate that units are training across the majority of the spectrum of urban operations. Most of the units questioned performed half of their urban training in lower intensity environment and the other half at the higher end of the spectrum. Some performed 75% high-intensity UO and only 25% low-intensity.[134] Every unit surveyed stated that they include civilians on the battlefield with a frequency ranging from some of the time to often. [135]

Urban training that is provided at the CTCs is conducted across the spectrum of intensity in their scenarios. For instance, the JRTC provides a lower-intensity scenario in the first two phases of normal rotations, escalating to a high-intensity urban scenario at the conclusion of the rotation.[136] This is the same plan for the other CTCs as well.

A disturbing trend in urban training however, is lack of units training on urban defensive tasks. History teaches us that any combat unit fighting in a city will almost certainly have to

---

[132] U.S. Army, FM 3-06 *Urban Operations*, 1-8.
[133] U.S. Army, FM 3-0 *Operations*, 1-15
[134] UO Survey results
[135] Ibid.
[136] Major Al Katz, interview with author, 17 Jan 2002.

retain it for some period of time, which means transitioning from the offense to the defense.[137]

Yet no unit surveyed had ever trained in urban defense tasks.[138] All of their urban training tasks

had been offensively focused. Even at the CTCs the UO training focus is offensive in nature. For

instance, a typical JRTC rotation's final mission is an assault on an urban complex. A unit's

rotation ends after it culminates in the offense, and units are never made to retain the city from an

enemy counter-attack.[139]

Another disturbing trend deals with unit's inability to recognize when a transition is

about to occur or has occurred in the urban operational spectrum. For example, units do poorly in

identifying when to change the level of intensity in urban operations at the CTCs. After fighting

in a SASO, low-intensity environment, units often fail to achieve a shift in their operational

approach and TTPs when assaulting an urban complex that is heavily defended. Instead they

continue to conduct operations without adjusting their ROE or changing their unit's mindset. The

outcome is initially a heavy expenditure of friendly casualties, an increased level of frustration,

and eventual attrition-style assaults employed resulting in large amounts of collateral damage and

civilian loss of life. Part of the problem results from units not training to recognize the shifts in

level of an operation's intensity. Instead their training focuses either solely on low-intensity, or

solely on high-intensity scenarios at a time.[140]

Further compounding this dilemma is that there has been a shift in TTPs for fighting in

cities. Our doctrine and TTPs for fighting in cities have been a polluted with an inculcation of

techniques from special operations and civilian SWAT teams.[141] Such techniques as precision

room clearance with four men entering rooms and stacking on walls before entering buildings

---

[137] CPTs John Miles and Mark Shankle, "Bradleys in the City," *Infantry Magazine*, May-June 1996, 7.

[138] UO Survey results

[139] Major Al Katz, interview with author, 17 Jan 2002.

[140] UO Survey results

[141] Thomas X. Hammes, "Preparing for Today's Battlefield," 57,58.

have now become the doctrinal TTPs in the new FM3-06.11.[142] The problem with these techniques is that they assume a secure perimeter, and that the enemy is not using explosives such as mines, hand-grenades, or RPG's, not to mention thermobaric weapons such as the RPO-A Schmel.[143] The four-man entry puts too many soldiers into a room too quickly, leaving them vulnerable to grenades, RPGs or Schmels.[144] Additionally the risk of fratricide increases dramatically when using this technique to clear deep into rooms.[145] Furthermore, techniques such as moving and stacking along walls are extremely dangerous. As demonstrated in Mogadishu, when bullets impact into walls they ricochet and travel along them. Because of this phenomenon, the Rangers learned to stay away from walls claiming, "stacking was for fire-wood, not soldiers assaulting buildings."[146]

While some argue that what is required is more time to train on these new TTPs, it would be better to maintain TTPs that can be easily adjusted to fit the spectrum within which one is operating.[147] The old technique of moving in rushes, and using two-man teams to initially enter a building and clear a room is still applicable. Rather than change the entire battle drill to fit the situation, what should be adjusted is the amount of covering fire and the use of either fragmentary grenades or stun grenades according to the level of UO intensity. Tasks should be kept simple and adjusted according to the threat rather than made complicated and inflexible to adjustment as the new precision techniques have done. This is of particular significance for conventional forces plagued with rapid personnel turnover and limited training time and resources.

While units are conducting UO training across the spectrum, there is a greater requirement for training in a manner that facilitates the identification of transitions within the

---

[142]U.S. Army, FM 3-06.11 *Combined Arms Operations In Urban Terrain.*
[143] Thomas X. Hammes, "Preparing for Today's Battlefield," 56.
[144] Ibid.
[145] Major Al Katz, phone interview with author, 17 Jan 2002.
[146] CSM Michael Hall and SFC Micheal T. Kennedy, "The Urban Area During Support Missions Case Study: Mogadishu," 569.
[147] Brett C. Jenkinson, "MOUT and The US Army: Give us Time to Train," available on-line at http://call.army.mil/products/ctc_bull/01-9/jenkinson.htm, 11 Feb 2002.

operational spectrum. Training for full spectrum operations requires much more than singularly-focused scenarios. Next training must include defensive tasks as well as offense, stability and support tasks. Finally TTPs and doctrine must be flexible to adjustment. One must take care not to become too focused on special operation and civilian police techniques that neither lend themselves to the realities of combat nor account for conventional forces' limitations.

Command Emphasis on UO Training

Appropriate level of command emphasis is important if an initiative is to gain the proper attention required. For this reason, the researcher examined the level of emphasis units were placing on UO. The results were mixed. While units did not specifically list UO on their Mission Essential Task Lists (METL), they did include the tasks attack and defend, of which UO is a subtask.[148] Every unit also included UO in their quarterly training guidance; a positive sign.

A more tangible measure of command emphasis however, is demonstrated by the amount of time spent training UO. As late as 1993, most Army units only conducted urban training once every 18 months.[149] The UO survey results determined that most Army units today spend about two weeks a year conducting urban training. Only one battalion surveyed reported it had spent 3-4 weeks in the last year training UO, and this was primarily due to it being a UO test unit. One unit claimed it had conducted less than a week of UO training at home-station in the last year, and only one reported it had conducted none. While this is better than a few years back, there is still room for improvement. Army units must move beyond mentioning UO training and start dedicating an appropriate amount of time training for UO. As a measure, one former battalion commander, states that units should spend at least 40% of their training time in the urban environment.[150]

---

[148] UO survey results.
[149] Karl W. Eikenberry, "Improving MOUT and Battle Focused Training." *Infantry* 83, no. 3 (May – June 1993): 36- 39.
[150] Thomas X. Hammes, "Preparing for Today's Battlefield," 57.

Operational Level UO Training

While UO doctrine has moved beyond the tactical level, training has not. The reason for this failure to improve is due largely to the lack of UO facilities and resources, both live and constructive. The Army lacks live facilities large enough to facilitate operational level urban training. With regards to simulations, the Battle Command Training Program (BCTP) does not possess the adequate software to facilitate urban warfare at the division and corps levels.[151]

Summary

The Army is still not prepared to fight in the urban environment without either sustaining heavy friendly casualties or causing excessive collateral damage and loss of civilian life, or both. While UO training is receiving greater attention throughout the Army, it is still not being done adequately in terms of jointness, combined arms, and full spectrum, nor above the tactical level.

To improve this will require first and foremost a DOD-level, UO executive agent to ensure services cooperate and maximize joint urban training opportunities and share urban training resources. It will also require a greater investment in facilities, both at home-station and at CTCs. In addition to improving our ability to fight as a joint and combined arms team, this will also provide opportunities to validate as well as develop emerging doctrinal concepts while determining resource requirements.

The Army must ensure it exercises the full spectrum of operations when conducting UO training. Most importantly training scenarios should be designed in a way that will train units to recognize and adapt to transitions in the urban operational environment. To be successful requires an easily understood, flexible ROE and simple, easily adjustable TTPs that can be performed by conventional forces. To do this, commanders must place greater emphasis on UO training starting with the allocation of an appropriate amount of time for such training. One way to achieve this is to make it mandatory for every training event to include UO events.

---

[151] CAMTF "Mission Need Statement For Urban Operations Training Capability,"A-7.

Now that doctrine has progressed beyond the tactical realm, so too must training. But first the Army must possess the infrastructure that supports this. In the next chapter, we will examine the state of the Army's infrastructure and how well its forces are resourced to conduct contemporary UO.

CHAPTER 6

RESOURCING THE FORCE FOR URBAN OPERATIONS

All the high-tech weapons won't transform our armed forces unless we transform the way we think, train and fight.

Donald Rumsfeld, US Defense Secretary

Introduction

In order for the Army to conduct effective urban operations it must be trained to do so, and for this training to be effective, it must be adequately resourced. Furthermore, units must possess the right equipment to fight and win in the unique urban environment. These two things, training and equipping, are inextricably linked to one another. Training helps determine the effectiveness of unit equipment, as well as assist in the designing of new systems. Units must possess the proper equipment in order to enhance learning, validate TTPs and doctrinal concepts, and accomplish missions.

The primary hindrance to the Army's progression in urban training and ability to conduct urban operations revolves around limited urban training facilities and lack of specific equipment for UO. While the Army has made improvements in their training facility infrastructure and developed a strategy for continued development of these facilities, these initiatives are not yet completed. In the meantime there is still much that can be done to capitalize on present facilities in order to maximize the Army's current UO capabilities.

Units are presently not equipped to adequately conduct UO effectively. While there are many technologically advanced programs being tested and examined, the force still does not possess the appropriate basic tools to conduct combat in cities. Many of these shortfalls require simple fixes, while solving others will require greater emphasis from the highest levels within DOD.

Training Facilities

The Army has focused its urban training on enhancing the capabilities of individual soldiers, and small unit collective tasks from squad to company level, which takes place primarily at home-station facilities.[152] Due to facility and land constraints, UO training above the company level usually does not occur at home-stations (see table 2.)[153]

Location of Facility	Number of Buildings	Number of Buildings Instrumented	Largest Unit Trained	Combined Arms Training	Live-fire Training
Ft Bragg	32	None	Company	No	No
Ft Hood	16	None	Platoon	No	No
Ft Hood	32	None	Company	No	No
Ft Campbell	8	None	Platoon	Yes	Yes
Ft Campbell	14	None	Company	No	No
Ft Drum	32	None	Brigade	Yes	Yes
Schofield Barracks, HI	16	4	Company	No	No
Ft Knox	21	10	Battalion	Yes	Limited
Ft Benning	32	6	Battalion	Yes	No
Hohenfels, GE (CTC)	37	None	Brigade	Yes	No
Ft Polk (JRTC)	26	26	Brigade	Yes	Yes
Ft Picket	16	None	Battalion	Yes	No
Ft McClellan	16	None	Battalion	Yes	No
Camp Blanding	16	None	Battalion	Yes	Yes
Camp Gruber	16	None	Battalion	No	No

Table 2. Existing Army Urban Training Facilities[154]

---

[152] GAO, *Military Capabilities: Focused Attention Needed to Prepare U.S. Forces for Combat in Urban Areas*, 10.
[153] Ibid.
[154] Ibid. 32.

One of the reasons for the neglect of urban training infrastructure was the Army's inability to overcome its focus on maneuver warfare in unrestricted terrain. As a result, urban training facilities (live, virtual, and constructive) have been under-funded for years and remain insufficient. For example, there is no urban training facility in Korea; one of our most likely contingency theaters that is densely urban.

According to survey results, most units rated their home-station urban training facilities as poor to inadequate. Only one respondent rated their facilities as adequate; none rated them as good. As previously mentioned, little combined arms training and no joint training occurs at these facilities as well.[155] Additionally the majority of these facilities are not instrumented and do not accommodate live-fire exercises, nor do they allow for dynamic breach training.[156] This breaching technique proved extremely useful in Grozny, allowing Russian soldiers to advance against the enemy within buildings, while avoiding exposure by moving in open streets.

Most of these facilities do not replicate the urban environments that soldiers are most likely to face. Instead of replicating cities in the Third World, most have been built to resemble small European villages. They normally possess a sterile environment, lacking trash, rubble, vehicles, and do not incorporate shantytowns or narrow streets that are prevalent in most Third World cities.

According to GAO investigators, urban training at battalion and brigade level has been reserved for the two CTCs, which possess urban training facilities (JRTC and CMTC.)[157] Training at these CTCs is usually only available to Army units once every 12 to 18 months and units only spend one 24-hour period out of a 12-day rotation fighting in the city.[158] During many

---

[155] UO Survey.
[156] Dynamic breaching is a breaching technique that uses explosives to create holes in walls or doors.
[157] GAO, *Military Capabilities: Focused Attention Needed to Prepare U.S. Forces for Combat in Urban Areas,* 10.
[158] Ibid.

rotations, some battalion-sized units never fight in the city, because they are either conducting cordon operations on the perimeter, or their combat power has been significantly reduced prior to reaching the city. Furthermore, of all the CTCs, only JRTC's facilities provide live-fire capability with full instrumentation.[159]

Presently, none of DOD's training facilities replicate the following challenges:

- The effects of medium and tall buildings, underground networks, and electromagnetic interference on communications equipment and navigation aids such as the global positioning system.

- Combat operations in medium or tall buildings.

- The difficulties in finding both stationary and mobile targets in the dense clutter of people, vehicles and buildings of a functioning city.

- Combat operations on unfamiliar terrain.[160]

The training these facilities accommodate does not provide the opportunity to test emerging doctrinal concepts such as maneuver warfare in cities and nodal attack. For instance, the size of the urban training facilities at both home-station and the CTCs do not exceed 40 buildings. Due to this limited size, units no higher than the brigade level are forced to engage in tactical-level, attrition warfare, because the facilities are not conducive to maneuver warfare within them. In addition, the small facilities do not present units with the challenge of getting lost inside of cities like TFR experienced in Mogadishu and the Russians did in Grozny. Compounding the live environment deficiencies is the lack of constructive infrastructure to assist in training operational-level maneuver warfare in cities.

There is good news however concerning the Army urban training facilities. The Combined Arms MOUT Task Force (CAMTF) has developed an Urban Operations Training Strategy for the improvement of urban training facilities. The strategy's endstate is to create a

---

[159] Ibid. 12.
[160] Ibid. 13.

doctrinally sound, operationally supported, live, virtual, and constructive training environment.[161] In order to implement this urban operations training strategy that is synchronized with the appropriate Theater strategy and associated force mix the, following objectives have been developed:

- Construct training facilities for forward deployed and heavy forces first.

- Construct brigade-level, urban training facilities at the CTCs, which will focus on battalion task forces.

- Construct regional combined arms facilities to support active and reserve forces.

- Construct soldier thru battalion-level training facilities at home station.

- Develop constructive simulations that support unit and staff training and leader development from battalion through corps…CTC and home station.

- Develop virtual simulators that train leader and team urban skills.[162]

Training facilities in the live environment will focus on brigade level UO training and below (see appendix A). The training will include individual and collective level tasks that will be performed at the Urban Assault Course (UAC), Breach Facility (BF), Live-fire Shoot House (SH), and a Combined Arms Collective Training Facility (CACTF).[163] To support these new facilities the CAMTF published TC 90-1, *Training for Urban Operations*, which outlines specifics on how to plan, resource, execute and evaluate UO training.

In addition to improving home-station training facilities, there will be upgrades to the CTCs with UAC, BF, SH, and CACTF facilities as needed. The biggest investment will be at the NTC by populating it with enough UO sites of varying sizes, to ensure that rotational units are always considering UO in their missions.[164] As a result, training at the NTC will no longer be conducted on a military-only battlefield, but will force units to deal with non-combatants, irregular forces, asymmetrical operations, and preservation of vital infrastructure in an urban

---

[161] CAMTF, "Mission Need Statement For Urban Operations Training Capability." Annex A, 8.
[162] Ibid.
[163] Ibid. 9.

environment.[165] With the addition of these UO sites, it is envisioned that the rotational brigades will have one attack mission into a brigade-sized complex and at least one mission that requires operations in and around one of the smaller UO sites.[166]

To fully develop leaders and ensure that forces from corps staff to the individual soldier are trained to as high a level as possible, the Army UO training infrastructure must contain the right blend of live, virtual, and constructive training (see appendix B.)[167] Current constructive simulations and virtual simulator capabilities are insufficient, which limits training for UO to the tactical level. Future capabilities for UO are to be provided by WARSIM and OneSAF (One Semi-Automated Force). WARSIM, as an aggregate based model, is limited by its level of terrain resolution to the exterior of buildings, but will be digitally linked with OneSAF providing a seamless simulated environment in which to train battalion through Corps.[168] When fielded, these systems will provide the much-needed infrastructure for operational-level UO training.

Before constructive operational infrastructure can be realized, work still needs to be done on the development of algorithms that take into account the effect of structural, environmental, people, and weapons' effects in complex terrain.[169] One of the pre-requisites for the development of these algorithms however, is the instrumentation of current training facilities in order to record data and develop models for individual human responses and small-unit behavior.[170]

Individual leader training at company level and below will be achieved through a combination of digitally linked virtual and live simulations. The virtual leader effects trainer (VLET) will provide the link between WARSIM/OneSAF to live training facilities, and will be

---

[164] G3, National Training Center, "Unpublished Concept Paper: NTC Urban Operations Training Requirements," 2 Oct 2000, 1.

[165] Ibid.

[166] Ibid., 3.

[167] CAMTF, "Mission Needs Statement For Urban Operations Training Capability," 3,4.

[168] Ibid.

[169] Ibid., Annex A, 15.

[170] Joint Advanced Warfighting Program, "Draft DOD Roadmap for Improving Capabilities for Urban Operations," 23.

integrated with the Close Combat Tactical Trainer (CCTT).[171] The implementation of these

integrated systems is to occur during the period from FY 03-09.[172] Once completed, the CAMTF

believes it will have achieved the UO training strategy's endstate, which is to create a doctrinally

sound, operationally supported, live, virtual, and constructive training environment, that will

enable the Army to train full spectrum, combined arms, and joint UO from corps staff to

individual soldier level.

UO Equipment

The US Army suffers from a significant number of shortfalls in the area of UO specific

equipment. As previously mentioned, this is directly related to the lack of focused attention

urban operations have received in the past. But even as UO receives more emphasis for future

technologically advanced programs, there will always remain a requirement for basic tools and

equipment for the conduct of urban warfare. Yet current forces are not even equipped properly

with these capabilities. Many of these shortfalls require high-level DOD emphasis for instance,

in the funding of programs for UO specific research and development. Other shortfalls simply

require focused command emphasis and small unit leadership ingenuity.

If one were to examine the technology employed by the Russians in Grozny in the 1990s,

they would find that it varied little from what was available prior to 1982.[173] Even the US forces

did not possess significant urban technological improvements in Mogadishu. Weapons used in

these battles were primarily the same as those developed for the open field of battle during the

Cold War. In some cases, ROE limited the stronger sides use of tanks and indirect fire

advantages and in both instances, neither non-lethal weapons nor precision-guided munitions

---

[171] Ibid., 14.
[172] Ibid.19.
[173] Edwards, *Mars Unmasked: The Changing Face of Urban Operations*, 89.

were employed.[174] As a result, small arms used in the close quarters were still the deciding factor in these urban fights.

Incidentally, superior technology is often times negated by very non-technical means. As example, in Mogadishu, barefoot SNA kept up with US HMMWVs and even orbiting helicopters by forcing the US to fight through multiple roadblocks and ambushes and use of the swarm technique.[175]   In Chechnya, the Russians resorted to using wire-mesh screens as a counter to RPG rounds and Molotov cocktails. When attacking, the Chechens employed such tactics as throwing tarps over armored vehicles' vision blocks, blinding buttoned up Russian crews.[176]

None of these concepts are new to urban warfare, however they are still challenges that must be dealt with. The solution for many of UO's challenges lie not in high-tech gadgetry, but can be mitigated through solid preparation and most importantly doctrine and training. FM 3-06.11 outlines a good start point for equipping units for urban combat (see appendix C). This UO equipment checklist does not include technically advanced equipment, and could be easily assembled by any unit in the Army.

Yet units surveyed suffered from a clear lack of even preparing such simple urban equipment kits as those outlined in the FM 3-06.11. Units reported to be mostly equipped with body armor, knee and elbow pads and some bolt cutters. Very few possessed such items as ladders, DEMTEK breach kits[177], assault wire and phones, additional communications equipment, or room cleared marking devices. Such kits as those listed in FM3-06.11 should be easy for tactical units to assemble and train or deploy with. This area clearly requires greater command emphasis for improvement.

Beyond units improving basic tools for urban warfare at their level, there is a requirement for DOD to re-examine current equipment shortfalls and requirements for ground forces in UO.

---

[174] Ibid.
[175] Ibid.
[176] Ibid.

The Army's current weapons and equipment are designed for armored, maneuver warfare. As far back as 1973, S.L.A. Marshall wrote that the geometric, man-made and structural limitations and confinement of fighting in streets and through houses are in diametric contrast to the requirements of operating in the open field.[178]

Many of the difficulties found in employing current weapon systems in UO are fairly well known.[179] For example artillery and mortars face trajectory challenges, are often too indiscriminate, and the impact of their rounds are too large to be used in close proximity of troops in urban areas. Tank rounds are designed for the penetration of other tank's armor and not useful for breaching into the walls of buildings. Small arms weapons such as the M16 possess a high muzzle velocity and project a small 5.56mm round that is prone to ricochet and lacks the ability to penetrate concrete walls.

To address these weapon shortfalls, the US is developing various high-tech systems. The Objective Individual Combat Weapon (OICW, to replace the M16, M4, and M203) and the Objective Crew Served Weapon (OCSW, to replace the 40mm MK-19, and the .50 caliber M2) are under development specifically with UO in mind.[180] These systems will include airbursting munitions to allow engagement behind cover or within rooms, and may also include non-lethal munitions.[181] However, these weapon systems are not scheduled for fielding until sometime starting in 2008.

Units surveyed consistently stated that the biggest weapons requirement they possessed for successful operations in UO was an urban missile that could conduct standoff breaching. Russian examinations of their UO in Chechnya concluded that their infantry must possess in the

---

[177] DEMTEK breach kits consist of mini-sledgehammers, hooligan tools, and crowbars for non-dynamic breaching into buildings.

[178] S.L.A. Marshall, "Notes on Urban Warfare," April 1973, 30.

[179] Russell W. Glenn, *Marching Under Darkening Skies: The American Military and the Improving Urban Operations Threat,* (Santa Monica, CA: RAND, 1998), 15.

[180] Ibid.

[181] Ibid.

direct fire mode, the same capabilities of those provided by indirect fire systems and tanks.[182]

S.L.A. Marshall supported this claim almost three decades ago stating,

> The U.S. Army has nothing now that will serve in the absence of field guns and mortars. The requirement is something by the way of a rocket that will range out to 200 meters.[183]

The Army needs to continue to develop a system to address this requirement. There are systems that will achieve the required effects of standoff breaching that should be rapidly increased in the Army's inventory for use in training and operational employment. One such system is the Shoulder Launched, Multipurpose, Assault Weapon, Disposable (SMAW-D); an 83mm rocket that can effectively breach walls and destroy bunkers.[184] Another system that has shown promise is the Rifle-Launched Entry Munition (R-LEM) used for breaching doors. After successful testing, it has been moved to the Warfighter Rapid Acquisition Program to hasten its fielding in the Army.[185]

Communications continue to be a shortfall for units fighting in cities. Once again, units surveyed often had no additional communications equipment beyond their standard authorized FM systems. This shortfall is primarily due to the limited and unrealistic challenges placed on unit's communications infrastructure in current training facilities. Realistic urban environments have proven communications to be difficult at best when using current systems. For example command posts usually located on lower floors for force protection must mount their antennas on rooftops. Yet standard antennas cannot be placed more than 3 stories above them without significant loss of signal strength.[186]

---

[182] Vyacheslav Dudka, "Shaping the Concept of Weapons For Urban Combat," *Military Parade*, 74.

[183] S.L.A. Marshall, "Notes on Urban Warfare" 26.

[184] US Army, FM 3-06.11, *Combined Arms Operations in the Urban Environment*, 7-17.

[185] Dr. A. Michael Andrews II, "The Army S&T Program" in *The City's Many Faces: Proceedings of the RAND Arroyo-MCWL-J8 UWG Urban Operations Conference*. Ed. Russell W. Glenn (Santa Monica: Rand, 1999), 30.

[186] Russell W. Glenn, *Combat in Hell: A Consideration of Constrained Urban Warfare*, (Santa Monica, CA: RAND): 29.

Another shortfall in UO involves the inability of dismounted infantry and supporting armor to effectively fight as a combined arms team. For instance the M-1 tank does not possess a dismounted phone hook up in the rear of the tank as did the M-60 it replaced. Instead, dismounted squads and tanks must rely on tenuous FM communications with each other when fighting as a combined arms team. Another example is dismounted forces inability to designate targets thermally for supporting tanks. Infantry designating systems utilize lasers that are not visible to tanks thermal sights.

The inability to provide maps with large enough scale for conducting UO continues to challenge the Army. The current 1:50,000 scale maps that are standard for conducting operations do not provide enough resolution for small units fighting at close quarters in cities. For example the British use a 1:4,000 scale map in urban ground operations, and units in the Berlin Brigade used a 1:1,500 scale map for UO in the defense of Berlin.[187] However, such large-scale maps may not be the answer, since they are not readily available and are impractical for aircrews flying in support of ground operations.[188] One potential fix is to provide units with the capability to receive overhead imagery of cities and then be able to overlay a grid system and to label selective key buildings and facilities.[189] This could easily be done using the latest MCS systems in conjunction with a division's topographical engineer section.

Units still lack to the ability to provide a rapid obscurant application over a wide area for a long period of time.[190] Most units surveyed still used hand-held smoke grenades and lugged a few smoke pots into the urban fight, which does not provide enough smoke for adequate cover of movement between buildings and crossing open areas. UO relies heavily on smoke screens to cover movement and is a resource intensive asset. For example, one-fifth of all artillery fired in

---

[187] Ibid.,32.
[188] Ibid.
[189] Ibid., 33.
[190] Russell W. Glenn, ed. *Denying the Widow-Maker: Summary of Proceedings,* (Santa Monica: CA, 1998): 23.

Chechnya was either smoke or white phosphorous.[191]   Smoke rounds were fired to screen movement, and white phosphorous had the additional effect of being lethal and incendiary.[192] Depending on ROE, this could be a potential vulnerability for light infantry units. Unless allowed to use phosphorous rounds or augmented with corps 155mm artillery, the only artillery delivered smoke that a light infantry unit possesses is provided by its 105mm artillery. Incidentally, the smoke munitions for 105mm can only achieve a range of 5,000 meters.[193]   What the Army needs is a small, heavily armored, maybe even remotely-piloted, ground vehicle that can provide ground units with adequate smoke coverage. S.L.A. Marshall identified this requirement almost 30 years ago, yet such a capability has yet to be developed.

Finally, another item that units need in today's urban environment is a sensory capability to scan civilians to determine if they have been involved in the firing of weapons. Lacking this capability, the Russians resorted to checking civilians' shoulders for bruises from weapons firing, or sleeves for powder signatures from mortar fire.[194] The U.S. possesses no better capability and have resorted to using dogs at select checkpoints for such sensing. Clearly in today's convoluted urban environment, such sensory technology is necessary to separate true civilians from urban guerrillas.

Summary

The US Army currently does not possess adequate urban training infrastructure to fully realize its combat potential across the spectrum of UO in a combined arms and joint manner. While the Army can continue to train effectively to company and some battalion level competency in UO tasks, there is still an outstanding requirement for facilities and infrastructure

---

[191]Lester Grau and Tim Thomas, " 'Soft Log' and Concrete Canyons: Russian Urban Combat Logistics in Grozny," (Fort Leavenworth, KS: Foreign Military Studies Office, 1999), 4. Report on-line. Available from http://call.army.mil/call/fmso/fmsopubs/issues/softlog/softlog.htm
[192] Ibid.
[193] US Army, A304 Handbook: *Fire Support For Non-artillerymen*, (Fort Leavenworth, KS: Command and General Staff College, 2001) 4-25.
[194] Tim Thomas, briefing presented on Grozny, March 2001.

(live, virtual, and constructive) that will enable training from the corps staff thru the individual soldier level.

The good news is that there has been continuous progress in strategy development and funding for the creation of a doctrinally sound, operationally supported, live, virtual, and constructive training environment. Although the full implementation of this strategy is not due to be completed until FY 2009, the Army must capitalize on the facilities it has in the meantime to achieve as much preparedness as possible. This will require command emphasis at all levels as well as a maximum amount of junior leader ingenuity and initiative.

The Army still suffers a significant number of shortfalls in the area of UO specific equipment. Many of these will require DOD-level emphasis and programs to improve research, development and funding. These programs must be advanced to the forefront of the Army's transformation agenda. Although technology should not be envisioned as a significant factor in the near-term enhancement of U.S. UO readiness many of the basic tools needed for conducting UO missions are not being resourced in most units.[195] This is in spite of the fact that they are easily obtainable. Units cannot afford to wait for the technological fix from some "higher authority." Instead they must seize the initiative and garner the tools that they require to effectively prosecute urban operations in the immediate future.

---

[195] Russell W. Glenn, ed. *Denying the Widow-Maker: Summary of Proceedings*, 21.

CHAPTER 7

CONCLUSIONS AND RECOMMENDATIONS

The urgent requirement for US Army preparedness in conducting urban operations is very real. As global urbanization continues to increase, the contemporary threat environment makes operations in cities impossible to avoid. It is not enough to speak of preparing for "future urban operations"; the future is here today and the Army must be prepared to engage in urban operations even as it moves towards the objective force. Being prepared means having current doctrine, realistic training programs and facilities, and appropriate equipment to ensure success on the urban battlefield when the time comes to fight there.

Doctrine

The Army's UO doctrine has undergone a long overdue re-write and is still being developed. It now must continue to be developed to permeate the Army's entire spectrum of combined arms doctrinal publications. For example, this includes addressing UO as it applies to specific battle operating systems, weapon systems, as well as marksmanship programs.

The Army's doctrine contains new concepts that attempt to solve UO dilemmas such as significantly reducing both friendly and civilian casualties, as well as collateral damage. While this UO doctrine possesses a new operational framework of Assess, Shape, Dominate, and Transition, it still provides a bridge between the gap in the Army's legacy force capabilities and those of the future objective force. In the near term, the Army must emphasize training and equipping to win in the domination phase of UO. At the same time greater ISR capabilities must be tested, funded, and implemented to improve the Army's ability to assess and shape the UO environment, thus facilitating the execution of operational maneuver concepts within the urban environment. Many of the new joint doctrine concepts, such as nodal attack, still require further testing to ensure they are valid as well as to develop service contributions. These initiatives should be the first priority of the joint executive agency, which should be activated immediately, not a year from now.

UO Training

Now that the Army's UO doctrinal foundation has been laid, the Army must continue to build its UO capabilities through training, organizing, and equipping the force for operating in the urban environment. The researcher determined that the Army is still not prepared to fight in cities without either sustaining heavy friendly casualties or causing excessive collateral damage and loss of civilian life, or both. While UO training is receiving greater attention throughout the Army, it is still not being done adequately in terms of jointness, combined arms, full spectrum, or above the tactical level.

Improving this will require first and foremost a DOD-level, UO executive agent to ensure services cooperate and maximize joint urban training opportunities and share urban training resources. It also requires a greater investment in facilities, both at home-station and at the CTCs. The facilities at the CTCs must be large enough to present units with realistic challenges such as navigating through cities, attacking in multiple directions, and employing joint assets. In addition to improving the Army's ability to fight as a joint team, this will also provide opportunities to validate and develop emerging doctrinal concepts while determining resource requirements.

The Army possesses a good strategy for improving home station training facilities, and must ensure adequate funding for both the construction and sustainment of these facilities. In the near term, heavy unit installations should be the first to receive these facilities, thus enhancing the opportunity for combined arms UO training. Additionally, light units must exploit every opportunity to train with heavy units in the urban environment both at home station and the CTCs.

The Army must ensure it exercises the full spectrum of operations when conducting UO training. Most importantly, training scenarios should be designed in a way that will train units to recognize and adapt to transitions in the urban operational environment. To achieve proficiency in this, commands need to apply greater emphasis on UO training, starting with the allocation of an appropriate amount of time for such training. One course of action is to make UO a mandatory occurrence during every training event. Another technique is to ensure training scenarios are designed to force commanders, leaders, and soldiers to recognize transitions in urban operations.

There has been a pollution of Army conventional forces' room clearing techniques with those used by police and special operations units. This disturbing trend advocates dominating a room with a 4-man clearing team. In addition, emerging urban movement techniques, which involve stacking on walls and moving in clusters are equally alarming. These TTPs could prove extremely fatal to soldiers fighting in an environment proliferated with RPG-7s and RPO-A Schmels, as well as mines, booby-traps, snipers and ricocheting rounds from small arms. In addition, the time required to master these techniques is not available to the conventional force. The Army must retain its conventional approach of clearing rooms with two-man teams and conduct forward movement through interior walls of buildings. When movement in the open is unavoidable, then it should be done in quick dashes under the cover of obscurants and fires.

Even if units avoid enemy strong points and attack key nodes within a city, at some point they must close with and destroy an enemy defending from a building. Precision weapons and guided munitions may assist, but will not be able to complete the destruction of an enemy in the UO environment. The Army must therefore continue to train on the basics to engage and destroy an enemy in the close fight in UO. Some of these basics include ensuring soldiers are physically fit, expert marksman in close-quarters combat, and thoroughly trained in medical skills (i.e. combat lifesavers.) Units should prefect these basics regardless of available urban training infrastructure. The urgency of the urban threat does not allow them to wait for perfect equipment and training facilities.

61

UO Resourcing

The researcher found that the US Army currently does not possess adequate urban training infrastructure to fully realize its combat potential across the spectrum of UO in a combined arms and joint manner. While the Army can continue to train effectively to company and some battalion level competency in UO tasks, there is still an outstanding requirement for facilities and infrastructure (live, virtual, and constructive) that will enable training from the corps staff through the individual soldier level.

The good news is however, that there has been much progress in strategy development and funding for the creation of a doctrinally sound, operationally supported, live, virtual, and constructive training environment. Although the full implementation of this strategy is not due to be completed until FY 2009, the Army must capitalize on the facilities it has in the meantime to achieve as much preparedness as possible. This will require command emphasis at all levels as well as a maximum amount of junior leader ingenuity and initiative.

The Army still suffers a significant number of shortfalls in the area of UO specific equipment. In particular the Army needs an urban missile or rocket that provides infantrymen with "pocket artillery" to compensate for the degradation of artillery, mortars and tanks' effects in the urban environment. In the interim, the Army must expedite the fielding and employment of the SMAW-D and R-LEM systems to facilitate breaching and forced entry into buildings.

Communication challenges must be overcome using both low-tech wire means and current off-the-shelf technology, while at the same time exploring new technology. Meanwhile the U.S. Army must leverage current technology, such as mounting antenna relays on UAVs and blimps to overcome urban communications challenges.

In addition to the programs listed above, there are several other pertinent UO resource requirements that demand immediate attention. The age-old challenge of troops communicating with tanks and designating targets for them must be solved immediately if the Army is to truly integrate tanks and dismounted infantry. A system for providing responsive obscurants for forces approaching and moving in cities must be developed. Units must be provided with the ability to pull down urban imagery and disseminate to forces on the ground to overcome inadequate maps. And finally, units must be provided with sensory technology to screen civilians on the battlefield for indications they have been involved in recent fighting (e.g. gunpowder and explosive signatures on clothing, and hands). Many of these shortfalls require DOD-level emphasis to improve research, development and funding, and must be advanced to the forefront of the Army's transformation agenda.

The author cautions against an over-reliance on technological fixes to UO challenges, however. Units cannot afford to wait for the technological fix, but instead must seize the initiative and garner the tools that are required to effectively prosecute urban operations in the immediate future. To prepare for the certain employment of US forces in urban environments, it is better to focus on doctrine and training with the current tools and resources available. Technology should not be envisioned as a significant factor in the near-term enhancement of UO readiness.

Summary

The Army's doctrine is current. What is required now is UO training conducted at every level capable in order to validate doctrine, learn how to fight, and develop needed equipment for urban operations. This must be ongoing even as improvements in facilities and equipment are not yet completed. BG (Ret) David Grange presents it the best with the following quote:

> You'll go to war the way you are today…not the way you want to be. Regardless of your shortages in personnel, the time that you have available to train, or the resources that you have on hand, you've got to get on with it.[196]

---

[196]David Grange, US Army (Retired), "Training and Readiness for Urban Operations" in *Capital Preservation: Preparing for Urban Operations in the Twenty-First Century*, ed. Russell W. Glenn (Santa Monica: Rand, 2001), 289.

Echoing in his challenge are the words of the French in Algiers some 50 years ago, "He who dies has lost; **in order to win, learn how to fight**. In battle death sanctions every fault."[197] The Army would be wise to heed these words.

---

[197] Jean Larteguy, *The Centurions*, (London, England: Hutchinson and Company, 1961), 318.

APPENDIX A
(CAMTF URBAN TRAINING FACILITIES)

Urban Assault Course (UAC). The UAC is a five station training facility that is designed to train individuals, squads, and platoons.

- Includes a two-story offense/defense building, grenadier gunnery, an underground trainer, and two individual through platoon task/technique training lanes.
- Does not include an instrumentation package,
- Includes a three-dimensional target package and a conventional live fire pop-up target package at the grenadier gunnery station.

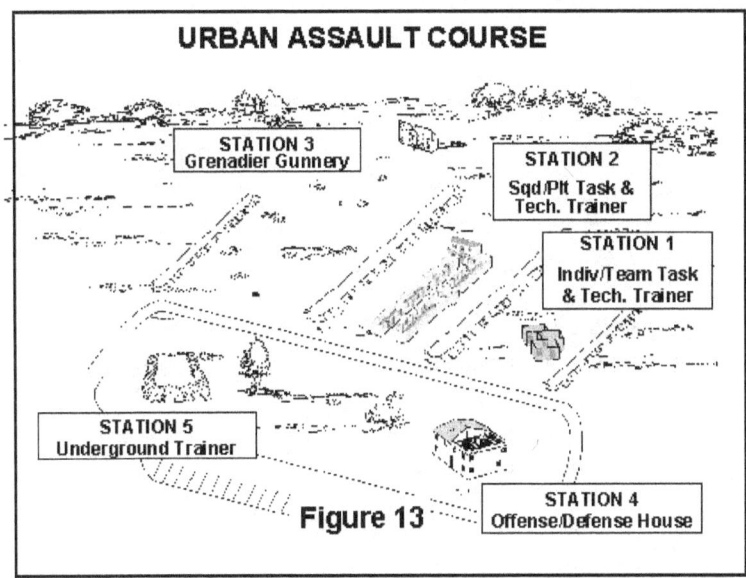

Figure 13

Live Fire Shoot House (SH). The SH is a single story building with multiple points of entry designed for individual, squad and platoon live fire training,

- Full audio/video instrumentation and portable after-actions review (AAR),
- Three-dimensional precision targetry packages.

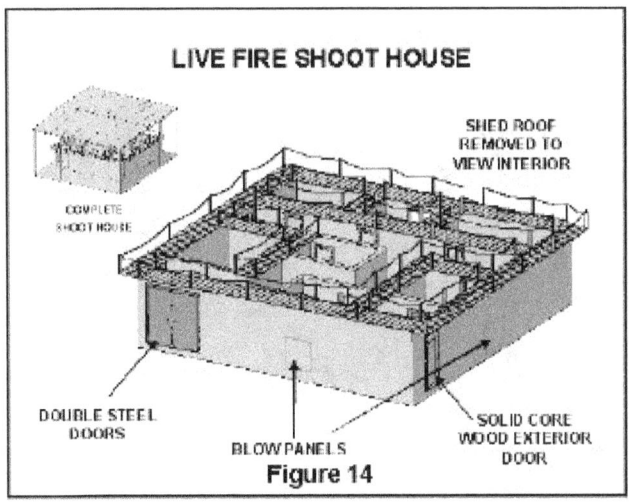

Figure 14

APPENDIX A
(CAMTF URBAN TRAINING FACILITIES)

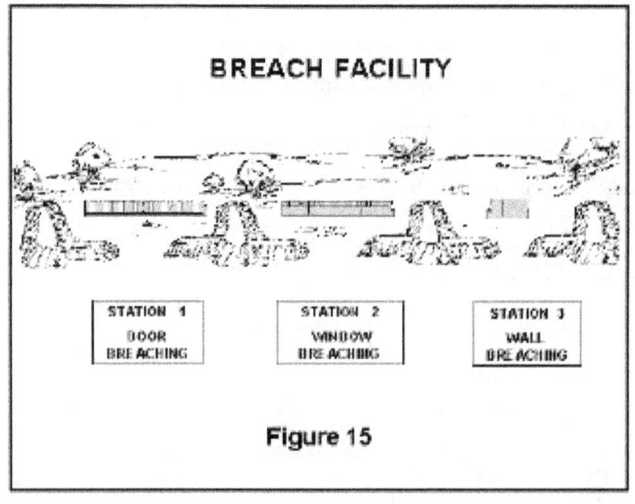

Figure 15

Breach Facility (BF). The BF is a training facility that includes wall, door, and window breach locations. The facility provides training for individual, teams and squads in breaching techniques and procedures. It trains the technical tasks of mechanical, ballistic, thermal, and explosive breaching.

- No instrumentation.

- Contains structural targetry only

Combined Arms Collective Training Facility (CACTF). The CACTF is a complex of 20-26 buildings covering an urbanized area of 2.25 square kilometers. The CACTF supports the training strategy as outlined in TC 90-1. The facility provides combined arms collective training for platoon and company situational exercises (STX) and battalion task force field training exercises (FTX).
- Audio/video capture instrumentation, three-dimensional precision targetry, AAR facility.
- Designed to accommodate expansion.

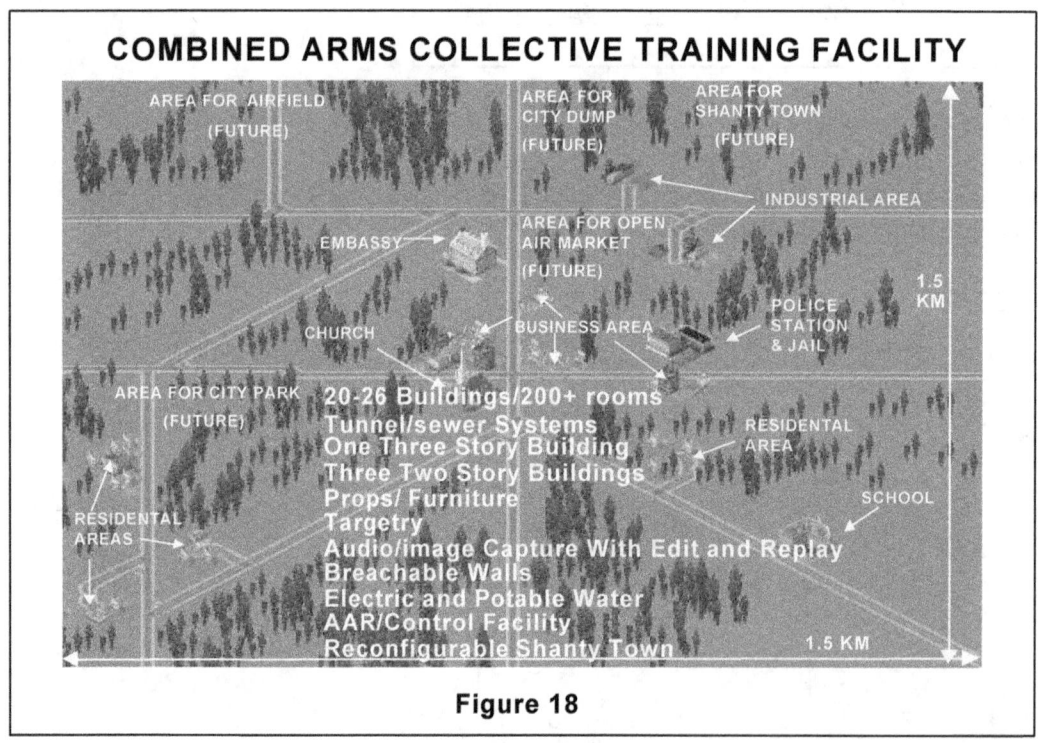

Figure 18

APPENDIX B
(FUTURE URBAN OPERATIONS TRAINING VENUES)

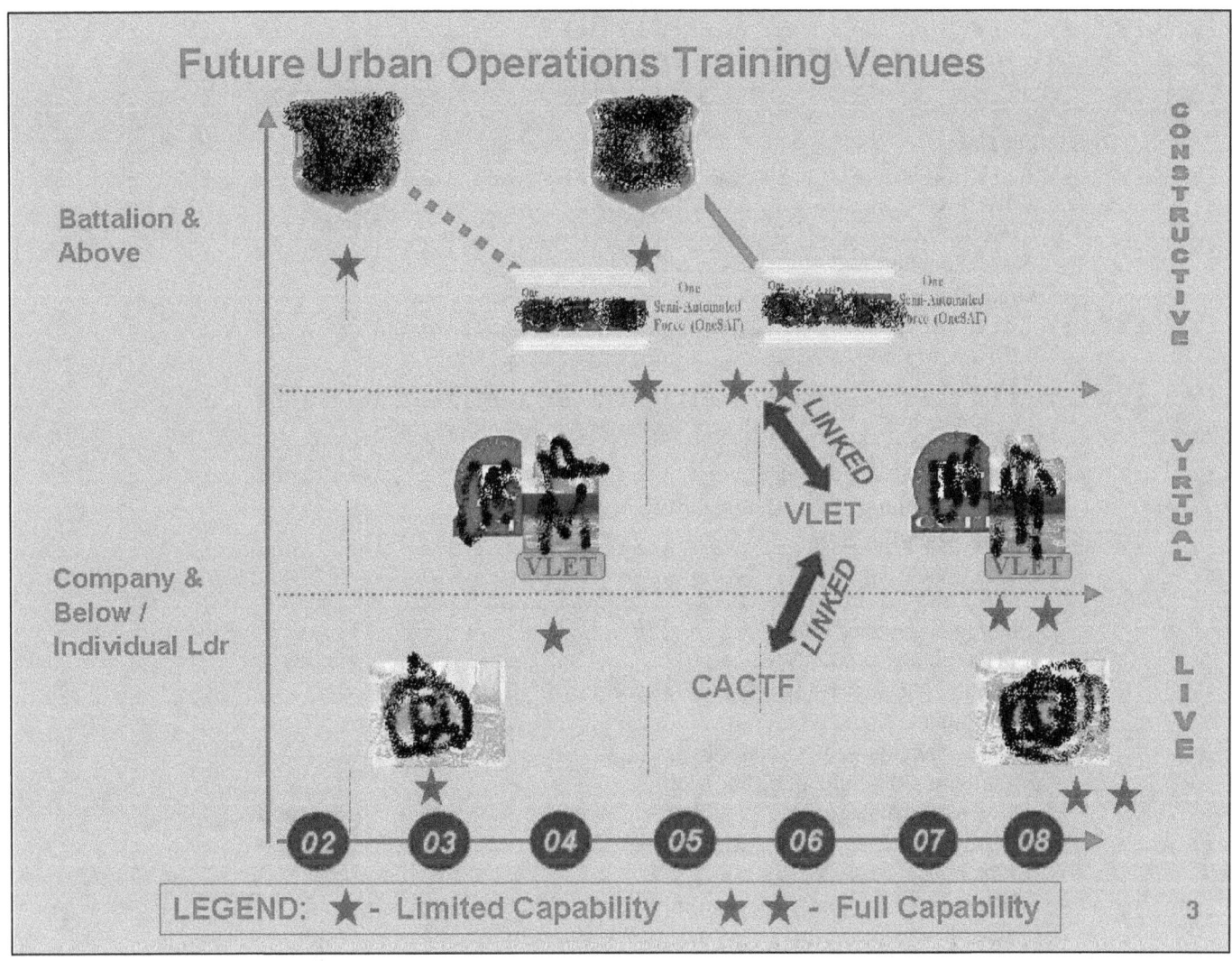

APPENDIX C
(PLATOON URBAN OPERATIONS KIT)[198]

Breaching Items:

     Axes...1
     Bolt cutters 2
     Crowbars..1
     Sledgehammers..1
     Grappling hooks 2
     120' nylon ropes..2
     12' sling ropes...4
     Snap links ....1 per man
     Lineman's pliers w/cutter 6
     Wire-handling gloves...3 pair
     Fireman's tool (hand pick-ax)..3
     Ladders (folding, collapsible, lightweight)........................1

Signaling and Marking Items:

     Chalk (large, sidewalk) ....2 boxes
     Spray Paint (assorted colors) ....5 cans
     Chemlites (assorted colors) ....3 boxes
     IR Chemlites..3 boxes
     Signaling mirrors (can be used for observing
          around corners) 6
     Cone flashlights w/extra batteries....................................12
     Flashlights (Magnum and Mini-Mag)
          w/extra batteries...1 per man
     NATO marking squares 200
     100mph tape ....5 rolls
     Masking tape..2 rolls
     2 sided tape ....3 rolls
     Engineer tape ....2 rolls

Other Items:

     Urban-specific sand table kit
     Hammers..2
     Saws 2
     Nails (various sizes) 4,000
     Steel wire (16 gauge)...1,000ft
     Hose clamps (6 inch) 300
     Extra batteries (various sizes)...3 additional for every
                                               one in use

---

[198] US Army, FM 3-06.11, *Combined Arms Operations in Urban Terrain*, appendix i.

NOTE: The preceding list of items and quantities is not all-inclusive or exclusive to urban operations. It is merely a guide to aid commanders in developing a standard platoon UO kit for their unit.

APPENDIX C
(PLATOON URBAN OPERATIONS KIT)

I-2. INDIVIDUAL PROTECTIVE EQUIPMENT

When planning for urban operations leaders must ensure that each soldier receives the following protective equipment in addition to standard TA-50 or unit issue items.

- Knee pads.
- Elbow pads.
- Eye protection.
- Hearing protection.

BIBILOGRAPHY

Books

Allard, Kenneth, *Somolia Operations: Lessons Learned*, Washington, D.C.: Defense University Press, 1999.

Bellamy, Christopher. *The Future of Land Warfare*. New York: St. Martin's Press, 1987.

Bolger, Daniel P. *Death Ground: Today's American Infantry in Combat*, Novato, CA: Presidio Press, 1999

Bowden, Mark. *Black Hawk Down: A Story of Modern War*. New York, NY: Penguin Books, 1999.

Collins, Arthur S., Jr. *Common Sense Training*. Novato, CA: The Presidio Press, 1978.

Clausewitz, Carl von. *On War*. Edited and Translated by Michael Howard and Peter Paret. Princeton, New Jersey: University Press, 1976

Dupuy, Trevor N. Col. USA (Ret.) and Col. Franklin D. Margiotta, USAF (Ret.), eds. *International Military and Defense Encyclopedia* (Washington, New York: Brassey's (US) Inc., 1993), s.v. "Urban Warfare" by Lutz Unterseher

Edwards, Sean J. A. *Mars Unmasked: The Changing Face of Urban Operations*. Santa Monica, CA: RAND, 2000.

Gerwehr, Scott. Editor. *The Art of Darkness: Deception and Urban Operations*. Santa Monica, CA: RAND, 2000.

Glenn, Russell W. Editor. *Capital Preservation: Preparing for Urban Operations In the Twenty-first Century: Proceedings of the Rand Arroyo-TRADOC-MCWL-OSD Urban Operations Conference*. Santa Monica, CA: RAND, 2000.

Glenn, Russell W. *Combat in Hell: A Consideration of Constrained Urban Warfare*. Santa Monica, CA: RAND, 1996.

Glenn, Russell W. Editor. *Denying the Widow-maker: Summary of Proceedings*. Santa Monica, CA: RAND, 1998.

Glenn, Russell W. Editor. *Heavy Matter: Urban Operations' Density and Challenges*. Santa Monica, CA: RAND, 2000.

Glenn, Russell W. Editor. *Marching Under Darkening Skies: The American Military and the Impending Urban Operations Threat.* Santa Monica, CA: RAND, 1998.

Glenn, Russell W. Editor. *The City's Many Faces: Proceedings of the Rand Arroyo-MCWL-J8 UWG Urban Operations Conference*. Santa Monica, CA: RAND, 2000.

Glenn, Russel W. *We Band of Brothers: A Call for Joint Operations Doctrine*, Santa Monica, CA: Rand, 1999.

Griffith, Samuel B. *Sun Szu: The Art of War.* London, England: Oxford University Press, 1963.

Hackworth, Col (Ret) David, *Hazardous Duty*, New York, NY: Avon Books, 1996.

Larteguy, Jean, *The Centurions*, London, England: Hutchinson and Company, 1961.

Matsumura, John. *Lighting Over Water: Sharpening Light Forces for Rapid Reaction Missions.* Santa Monica, CA: RAND, 2000.

Nolan, Keith William. *The Battle for Hue: Tet 1968.* Novato, CA: The Presidio Press, 1996.

Oliker, Olga, *Russia's Chechen Wars, 1994-2000: Lessons from Urban Combat,* Santa Monica, CA: RAND, 2001.

Peters, Ralph. *Fighting For The Future: Will America Triumph?* Mechanicsburg, PA: Stackpole Books,1999.

Rosen, Stephen P. *Winning the Next War.* New York: Cornell University Press, 1991.

Scales, Robert H. *Firepower In Limited War*. Novato, CA: The Presidio Press, 1995.

Scales, Robert H. *Future Warfare Anthology.* Pennsylvania: United States Army War College, 1999.

Simpkin, Richard E. *Race to the Swift: Thoughts on Twenty-First Century Warfare*. London: Brassey's Defense Publishers, 1985.

Spiller, Roger J. *Sharp Corners: urban Operations at Century's End.* Fort Leavenworth, KS: Combat Studies Institute, 2001.

Vick, Alan. *Aerospace Operations in Urban Environments: Exploring New Concepts.* Santa Monica, CA: RAND, 2000.

Articles and Periodicals

Boatman, John and Barbara Starr. "USA Looks For Answers to the Ugliness of Urban Warfare." *Janes Defence Weekly* (16 October 1993): 25.

Boyco, Robert G. "Just Cause MOUT: Lessons Learned." *Infantry* 81, no. 3 (May –Jun 1991): 28-32.

Brill, Arthur P. Jr. " More Likely Than Everest: USMC Hones Its Urban-Warfare Combat Skills." *Sea Power* 42, no. 3 (March 1998): 44-47.

Brown, Capt. Kevin W. "The Urban Warfare Dilemma – U.S. Casualties vs. Collateral Damage," *Marine Corps Gazette* 81, no. 1 (January 1997): 38.

Cameron, Robert S. "It Takes a Village To Prepare for Urban Combat…and Fort Know Is Getting One." *Armor* 106, no. 6 (November – December 1997): 9-12.

"Concept for Future Military Operations on Urbanized Terrain." *Marine Corps Gazette* 81, no. 10 (October 1997): A1-6 (following p. 44).

Dudka, Vyacheslav, "Shaping the Concept of Weapons For Urban Combat," *Military Parade*, 74.

Eikenberry, Karl W. "Improving MOUT and Battle Focused Training." *Infantry* 83, no. 3 (May – June 1993): 36- 39.

Geibel, Adam. "Lessons in Urban Combat: Grozny, New Year's Eve, 1994." *Infantry* 85, no. 6 (November – December 1995): 21-25.

Glenn, Russell W. "Fox Trot: Seeking Preparedness for Military Urban Operations." *Armed Forces Journal International* 136, no. 10 (May 1999): 46, 48-49.

Grau, Lester and Tim Thomas, " 'Soft Log' and Concrete Canyons: Russian Urban Combat Logistics in Grozny," (Fort Leavenworth, KS: Foreign Military Studies Office, 1999), 4. Report on-line. Available from http://call.army.mil/call/fmso/fmsopubs/issues/softlog/softlog.htm

Grimes, Vincent P. "New Urban Battlefield Calls for Body Armor." *National Defense* 80, no. 509 (July – August 1995): 36-37.

Hahn, Robert F. II and Bonnie Jezior. " Urban Warfare and the Urban Warfighter of 2025." *Parameters* 29, no. 2 (Summer 1999): 74-86.

Hammes, Thomas X. "Time To Get Serious About Urban Warfighting Training." *Marine Corps Gazette* 83, no. 4 (April 1999): 19-21.

Hewish, Mark and Rupert Pengelley. "Warfare in the Global City: The Demands of Modern Military Operations in Urban Terrain." *Jane's International Defense Review* 31, no. 6 (June 1998): 32-35, 38, 40-43.

Hillen, John. "Must US Military Culture Reform." *Parameters* 29 (Autumn, 1999): 9-23.

Hoffman, Jon T. "Marines Assault the Joint Readiness Training Center." *Marine Corps Gazette* 83, No. 2. (February 1999): 34-36.

Ide, Douglas. "Urban Combat Training." *Soldiers* 50, no. 12 (December 1995): 40-41.

Jenkinson, Brett C. "MOUT and The US Army: Give us Time to Train," available on-line at http://call.army.mil/products/ctc_bull/01-9/jenkinson.htm, 11 Feb 2002.

Koch, Andrew. "New Urban Warfare Centre Planned." *Jane's Defence Weekly*, 8 September 1999, 8.

Lieven, Anatol. "The World Turned Upside Down: Military Lessons of the Chechen War." *Armed Forces Journal International* 136, no. 1 (August 1998): 40, 42-43.

Miles, John and Shankle, Mark, "Bradleys in the City," *Infantry Magazine*, May-June 1996, 7.

Naylor, Sean D. "Lack of City Smarts? War Games Shows Future Army Unprepared Urban Fighting." *Army Times*, 11 May 1998, 22.

_____. "The Urban Warfare Challenge." *Army Times*. 15 April 1996, 12-14.

Panton, Jefferson R. "Company Team Offensive Operations in Urban Terrain." *Armor* 102, no. 6 (November – December 1993): 21-25.

Peters, Ralph. "The Future of Armored Warfare." *Parameters* 26, no. 1 (Spring 1996): 43-50.

Podlesny, Robert E. "MOUT: The Show Stopper." *US Naval Institute Proceedings* 124, no. 2 (February 1998): 50-54.

Rupe, Chad A. "The Battle of Grozny: Lessons for Military Operations on Urbanized Terrain." *Armor,* 08, no. 3 (May – June 1999): 20-23, 47.

Reynolds, John H. "A Case for 21st Century MOUT Facilities." *Marine Corps Gazette* 84, no. 7 (July 2000): 41-45.

Richardson, William R. "Training: Preparation for Combat." *Military Review* (April 1998)

Scales, Robert H. Jr. "Indirect Approach: How US Military Forces Can Avoid the Pitfalls of Future Urban Warfare." *Armed Forces Journal International* 136, no. 3 (October 1998): 68, 71-72, 74.

Stewart, Douglas. "MOUT Battle Drills for Infantry and Tanks." *Infantry* 83, no 3 (May – June 1993):40-42.

Sullo, Mark A. "Combat Decision Range Training." *Marine Corps Gazette* 83, no. 2 (February 1999):37-38.

Thomas, Timothy L. "The Battle of Grozny: Deadly Classroom for Urban Combat." *Parameters* 29, No 2 (Summer 1999): 87-102.

Valceanu, John. "Concrete Combat." *Soldiers* 54, no 6 (June 1999):41-45.

Wood, David. "U.S. Soldiers Ill-Prepared for Urban Combat Some Vets Say." *Army Times*, 19 April 1999, 16.

Villella, Susan, "Urban Evasion – A Necessary Component of Urban Operations," *JSSA SERE Newsletter*, October 1998, *http://www.geocities.com/Pentagon/6453/urbanevasion.html*,

2/23/02.

Zachau, John S. "Military Operations on Urban Terrain." *Infantry* 82, no. 6 (November – December 1992): 44-46.

<u>Government Documents</u>

Defense Science Board, *Report of the Defense Science Board Task Force on Military Operations in Built-Up Areas (MOBA),* Washington, D.C.: Office of the Under Secretary of Defense for Acquisition and Technology, 1994.

G3, National Training Center, "Unpublished Concept Paper: NTC Urban Operations Training Requirements," 2 Oct 2000

Joint Advanced Warfighting Program. "Draft DOD Roadmap for Improving Capabilities for Urban Operations", 20 November 2001

United Kingdom Ministry of Defence, *Army Field Manual: Operations in Special Environments.* Volume IV, Part 5: "Operations in Built-Up Areas (OBUA)," Stationary Office, 1998.

U.S. Army. A304 Handbook: *Fire Support For Non-artillerymen*, Fort Leavenworth, KS: Command and General Staff College, 2001.

_____. FM 3-0 *Operations.* Washington, D.C.: Department of the Army, 2001.

_____. U.S. Army, FM 3-06, *Urban Operations.* Washington, D.C.: Department of the Army, 2002.

_____. FM 3-06.11, *Combined Arms Operations In Urban Terrain.* Washington D.C.: Department of the Army, 2002

_____. ARTEP 7-10-MTP, *Mission Training Plan for the Infantry Battalion.* Washington DC: Department of the Army, 1997.

_____. ARTEP 7-20-MTP, *Mission Training Plan for the Infantry Battalion.* Washington DC: Department of the Army, 1997.

_____. ARTEP 7-30-MTP, *Mission Training Plan for the Infantry Brigade (Command and Staff).* Washington DC: Department of the Army, 1997.

_____. ARTEP 71-2-MTP, *Mission Training Plan for the Armored and Mechanized Infantry Battalion.* Washington DC: Department of the Army, 1997.

_____. FM 7-20, *The Infantry Battalion.* Washington DC: Department of the Army, 1992.

_____. FM 7-30, *The Infantry Brigade.* Washington DC: Department of the Army, 1995.

_____. FM 25-100, *Training the Force.* Washington DC: Department of the Army, 1988.

_____. FM 25-101, *Battle Focused Training*. Washington DC: Department of the Army, 1990.

_____. FM 71-2, *The Armored and Mechanized Infantry Battalion*. Washington DC: Department of the Army, 1996.

_____. FM 71-3, *The Armored and Mechanized Infantry Brigade*. Washington DC: Department of the Army, 1996.

_____. FM 90-10-1, *An Infantryman's Guide to Combat in Built-Up Areas*. Washington DC:Department of the Army, 1993.

_____. FM 90-13-1, *Combined Arms Breaching Operations*. Washington DC: Department of the Army, 1994.

_____. FM 100-5, *Operations*. Washington DC: Department of the Army, 1993.

US Department of Defense. Joint Publication 1-02, *Department of Defense Dictionary of Military and Associated Terms*. Washington DC: Government Printing Office, 1994.

U.S. Department of Defense. Joint Publication 3-06, *Doctrine for Joint Urban Operations*. Final Draft, 2002.

US Marine Corps. *Military Operations on Urbanized Terrain*. Washington DC: Government Printing Office, 1998.

US General Accounting Office. GAO/T-NSIAD-99-92, *Military Readiness: Full Training Benefits From Army's Combat Training Centers Are Not Being Realized*. Washington DC: Government Printing Office, 1999.

US General Accounting Office. GAO/NSIAD-00-63NI, *Military Capabilities: Focused Attention Needed to Prepare U.S.Forces For Combat in Urban Areas*. Washington DC: Government Printing Office, February 2000.

US Training and Doctrine Command, *The Future Operational Environment*, Unpublished White Paper, 4 May 2001.

Monographs, Reports, Theses, and Unpublished Works

Boynton, Frank R. *Power Projection Operations and Urban Combat: An Avoidable Combination?* Monograph, School of Advanced Military Studies. Fort Leavenworth, KS: US Army Command and General Staff College, 1995.

Bendewald, Gregory. *Required Operational Capabilities for Urban Combat.* Masters Thesis, Naval Postgraduate School. Monterey, CA, 2000.

Day, Clifford E. *Critical Analysis on The Defeat of Task Force Ranger.* Research Paper, Air Command and Staff College. Maxwell, AFB, 1997.

Dyer, J. L. *Light Infantry Performance at the Combat Training Centers: Home-Station*

Determinants. Research Report 9233, Army Research Institute Field Unit at Fort Benning, GA, 1992.

Everson, Robert E. *Standing at the Gates of the City: Operational Level Actions and Urban Warfare.* Monograph, School of Advanced Military Studies. Fort Leavenworth, KS: US Army Command And General Staff College, 1995.

Goligowski, Steven P. *Future Combat in Urban Terrain: Is FM 90-10 Still Relevant?* Monograph, School of Advanced Military Studies. Fort Leavenworth, KS: US Army Command and General Staff College, 1995.

James, William T. *From Siege to Surgical: The Evolution of Urban Combat from World War II To The Present and Its Effect on Current Doctrine.* Thesis, Master of Military Arts and Science. Fort Leavenworth, KS: US Army Command and General Staff College, 1998.

Kendrick, Scott T. *Urban Combat: Is the Mounted Force Prepared to Contribute?* Monograph, School of Advanced Military Studies. Fort Leavenworth, KS: US Army Command and General Staff College, 1991.

Kennedy, John R. "Players or Spectators? Heavy Forces Doctrine for MOUT." Monograph, School of Advanced Military Studies. Fort Leavenworth, KS: US Army Command and General Staff College, 1990.

Kirkland, Donald E. *Offensive Operations in Urban Europe: The Need for a "Heavy" Light Infantry Force.* Monograph, School of Advanced Military Studies. Fort Leavenworth, KS: US Army Command and General Staff College, 1985.

Marshall, S.L.A. *Notes on Urban Warfare.* Aberdeen Proving Ground, MD: Army Material Systems Analysis Agency, 1973.

Megahan, Rick. *Dragon in the City: Joint Power Projection and Joint Urban Operations – An Unavoidable Situation in the Near Future.* Thesis, Carlisle Barracks, PA: US Army War College, 1999.

Mosher, Alan M. *Light Armor MOUT Doctrine: Imperative Change or Business as Usual?* Monograph School of Advanced Military Studies. Fort Leavenworth, KS: US Army Command and General Staff College, 1994.

Odeen, Philip A. Panel Chairman *Transforming Defense: National Security in the 21ˢᵗ Century.* Report, Arlington, VA: National Defense Panel, December 1997.

Webster, William G, Jr. *Using U.S. Army National Training Center (NTC) Lessons Learned to Improve Combat Readiness.* Master of Military Art and Science. Thesis, US Army Command and General Staff College, 1984.

Wood, David. *The United States Army's Preparedness To Conduct Urban Combat: A Strategic Priority.* Thesis, Carlisle Barracks, PA: US Army War College, 1997.

Worley, Robert D. *Challenges to Train, Organize, and Equip the Complete Combined Arms Team: The Joint Task Force.* Report, Institute for Defense Analyses, Alexandria, VA,